SOLUTIONS FOR PROFITABILITY

SPIRO BUSINESS GUIDES
BUSINESS SKILLS

Spiro Business Guides are designed to provide managers with practical, down-to-earth information, and they are written by leading authors in their respective fields. If you would like to receive a full listing of current and forthcoming titles, please visit www.spiropress.com or email spiropress@capita-ld.co.uk or call us on +44 (0)870 400 1000.

SOLUTIONS FOR PROFITABILITY

PATRICK J. CORDON

First published in 2003 by
Spiro Press
17–19 Rochester Row
London
SW1P 1LA
Telephone: +44 (0)870 400 1000

© Patrick J. Cordon 2003

ISBN 1 904298 58 3

Reprint 2004

British Library Cataloguing-in-Publication Data.
A catalogue record for this book is available from the British Library.

All rights reserved. No part of this publication may be reproduced, stored in a retrieval system or transmitted, in any form or by any means, electronic, mechanical, photocopying, recording and/or otherwise without the prior written permission of the publishers. This book may not be lent, resold, hired out or otherwise disposed of by way of trade in any form, binding or cover other than that in which it is published without the prior written consent of the publishers.

Disclaimer: This publication is intended to assist you in identifying issues which you should know about and about which you may need to seek specific advice. It is not intended to be an exhaustive statement of the law or a substitute for seeking specific advice.

Spiro Press USA
3 Front Street, Suite 331
PO Box 338
Rollinsford NH 03869
USA

Typeset by: Turn-Around Typesetting, UK
Printed in Great Britain by: Digital Books Logistics Ltd
Cover design by: REAL451

Spiro Press is part of The Capita Group Plc

This book is dedicated to Jesus Christ, Lord and Saviour of the world.

Contents

Preface	xi
About the author	xiii

1	**Introduction**	**1**
	A global capital market system	3
	The supply chain into 2005	5
	International expansion	6
	The impact of technology	7
	What is competitive advantage?	9
2	**An approach to profitability**	**13**
	What is profitability?	14
	The six steps to profitability	19
	Core management components	23
3	**Self-assessment**	**27**
	What you have to know and do	28
	Indicators of a strong business	31
	Case study 3.1 ABC Manufacturing	40

4	**Business turnaround**	**49**
	Companies susceptible to trouble	50
	When a business turnaround may work	54
	Productivity	56
	Time	59
	Profit	62
	Getting started	62
	Case study 4.1 ABC Bakery Supply	67
5	**Supporting changes in the business**	**75**
	Developing a leadership team	79
	Typical reactions to change	80
	Strategies for changing systems	81
	Decision making	82
	Products and services	84
	Metrics	85
	Strategic measurement model: key factors	87
	Seven ways to make sure your measurement system fails	89
6	**Balanced scorecards**	**91**
	Balanced scorecards	92
	Developing metrics for your organisation's balanced scorecard	115
	Measuring customer satisfaction and value	118
	Measuring product and service quality	119
	Measuring processes and operational performance	121
	Measuring supplier performance	122
	Measuring employee satisfaction	124

	How to design your own measurement system	125
	Mission statements and vision statements	129
	Key success factors	130
7	**Your marketing plan**	**141**
	Marketing	141
	Market definition	143
	What is a marketing plan?	145
	Why a marketing plan is valuable to you	146
8	**Developing a market plan**	**151**
	Executive summary	151
	External environment analysis	152
	Organizational environment assessment	161
	Development of goals and objectives	166
	Strategy development	168
	Writing your marketing plan	175
	Developing a focused sales strategy	177
	Some keys to success	185
	What is active sales management?	187
	Taking your company into the international marketplace	191
9	**Product realization**	**199**
	Costs involved in the design process	199
	Cost databases and quality function deployment	200
	Current processes and their capabilities	201
	The market needs	203
	The benefits of cellular manufacturing	203

	Analysing your business for synchronous manufacturing	206
	Product realization	217
10	**Lean business system self-assessment**	**219**
	The purpose of self-assessment	219
	Using the self-assessment questionnaire	220
	Lean business system self-assessment: results analysis	229
	Integrating manufacturing planning and control systems into the supply chain	232
11	**Profitability analysis**	**239**
	Why prepare a profitability improvement plan?	239
	How your profitability plan can help you	240
	Who uses profitability improvement plans?	242
	Components of the profitability improvement plan	243
12	**Conclusion**	**259**

Appendices

A	Product realization checklist	265
B	Cost savings analysis	273

Preface

The profitability analysis concept has its basis in understanding and eliminating costs and improving margins in a business process. Profitability is the key component in any healthy business; the aim of this book is to help companies realize their profit potential and success through systematic approaches to profit improvement by giving them experience-based answers to operational and financial profitability questions.

Solutions for Profitability provides a stand-alone guide for anyone in need of a reference for business turnaround and profitability improvement. Although it provides a complete reference for the CEO/business turnaround analyst, it also provides guidance to management consultants, business managers and financial analysts who use or need to understand business turnaround methods. It is a process approach to profit improvement, one that focuses on core processes to improve your profits. It is written to ensure its content is equally applicable to all business turnaround activities and organizations.

Economic slowdowns and recessions come in all sizes and shapes. In most instances, however, their impact on sales is actually relatively modest. The problem is that even a modest drop in sales penetrates into profitability through the company, resulting in dramatically reduced profits or even losses.

This book provides a plan/roadmap and corresponding tools and strategies to improve profitability as well as hands-on checklists to guide the business user through the profitability improvement process. It explains how to rethink and rebuild the business from the bottom up, regardless of the prevailing economic conditions. This book is designed to provide accurate and authoritative information in regard to the subject matter covered. However, it is provided with the understanding that neither I nor the publisher is engaged in rendering legal, accounting or other professional services. If legal or other expert assistance is required, the services of a competent professional should be sought.

All good business owners and managers know they should have a solid, working business analysis plan in place. But the truth is that a business owner or manager will never achieve real success unless he draws a map of how he plans to get there. That map or business analysis plan will provide direction on how to move toward attaining business goals and, ultimately, success. A well-developed plan also helps when a business encounters sharp curves in the road, a bumpy stretch of highway or even a pothole that temporarily derails its progress. While these road conditions may impede success, they need not be devastating. By thinking about contingency plans while preparing a strategic business analysis plan, a business owner or manager can be prepared to handle any of the ups and downs of the business world.

About the author

Pat Cordon has completed, over the last 25 years, full business assessments for over 2,000 companies in die building, distribution, manufacturing and logistics, working with client management and business management systems. His background includes 23 years of financial/operational auditing, as well as training and managing operations auditors. He has also served in senior management positions with Proudfoot Crosby and the Steel Service Center Institute and management positions with the LTV Steel Company. He is a certified RAB/IRCA quality systems lead auditor for ISO 9001: 2000, an IATCA senior auditor, a RAB registered audit verifier, a RAB technical reviewer, an AIAG QS-9000/ISO 17025 certified auditor, an IATF ISO TS 16949 certified auditor and a QS-9000-TE certified auditor, as well as being an ICBC certified business counsellor who received his BA from Saint Vincent Colleage and his MBA in Industrial Management from Columbia Pacific University. In addition, he provides financial/operational auditing and system implementation for manufacturing/distribution/logistics companies worldwide.

Pat is married with three children and one grandchild.

The author may be contacted at:

590 Barrett Road
Berea
Ohio 44017
USA
Tel: +1 440 816 9081
E-mail: patrickcordon@aol.com
Website: http://www.patrickcordon.com

CHAPTER 1

Introduction

Forty-five years ago, American industrial strength was the best in the world. Fortified by a strong manufacturing base, a vast reservoir of technical expertise, and the temporary weakness of Europe and Japan, the USA dominated the global economy. The USA, following the Second World War, accounted for roughly half of the world gross national product. Since 1950, the US economy has adapted to some big changes:

- The 1950s saw the economy shift from a war to peace-time basis, then explode as the country tried to satisfy pent-up demand.

- The 1960s saw a rapidly expanding consumer economy and an overhaul of the nation's infrastructure. Additional rapid growth was caused by a major expansion in the use of metal. Complicating this picture for US producers was the growth of imported products from 4 to 14 per cent of domestic consumption.

- An erratic marketplace with significant inflation, stagnation and a rollercoaster ride of alternating growth and recession periods marked the 1970s.

- The 1980s saw a maturing US economy. Financial markets created new capital sourcing opportunities and the economy enjoyed an eight-year period of uninterrupted growth. However, consumption had actually declined by the end of the decade and import penetration increased to 26 per cent, reaching as high as 50 per cent in some product lines.

- In the 1990s American business (particularly medium- and small-sized businesses) experienced a highly charged, competitive environment identified by issues including: changing product markets; management of investments and assets; profit margin pressure; complex issues in cost control; appreciable capital and technological investment; lower skilled workforce; global partnerships; complex customer–auditor relationships; greater competitive intensity; significant consolidation; fragmentation of the marketplace and an influx of niche competitors, causing companies to carry narrower or broader lines to meet changing customer needs; more demanding customers; more emphasis on accurate financial, operational and quality reporting; a greater need for compliance with applicable laws and regulations; higher costs of doing business; the difficulty of finding and keeping good employees; a push for increased quality and productivity; uncertain and in some cases unreliable supply; rapidly expanded and costly value-added service requirements to maintain market share to meet increasing customer demands; and the difficult transition from national to global capital markets.

A global capital market system

Powerful strategic forces are driving the globalization of business, the worldwide integration of financial markets, and the growing interdependence among national and regional economies. Sophisticated observers believe that these trends are irreversible. A new-world political paradigm of reciprocity has emerged. Consider the following:

The European Monetary Union (EMU), the North American Free Trade Agreement (NAFTA) and the Association of Southeast Asian Nations (ASEAN) provide overwhelming evidence that a growing number of sovereign nations are subordinating some of their national policies and goals to regional agreements. The de facto enforceability of harmonized regional policy structures and controls is, without doubt, a major global breakthrough in the new millennium.

Innovative technologies and the huge breakthroughs in information technology (IT) over the past three decades are an everyday fact for hundreds of millions of people. Satellite and fibre optic technology permits global communications at high speed and low cost. These technological advances have contributed greatly to global interdependence. Two specific consequences are (1) the rise of the multinational corporation and (2) borderless financial markets.

Multinational corporations (MNCs) – multinational, transnational, international, global, stateless – no matter what the descriptor, these enterprises view the entire world as one market in which to produce and sell goods and services. Multinational corporations have become the most effective international transfer agents ever known, and all indications are that they have become a permanent feature of the world economy.

Cross-border deal making has meant that the terms mergers and acquisitions (M&A) have assumed new meaning and significance. Hardly a week goes by without an announcement of yet another cross-border merger. Shareholders appear to support cross-border deals. Regulators, by and large, seem to have few objections and consumers also appear supportive.

While most recognized markets are becoming increasingly global, this is especially true for financial markets. There is now an almost autonomous world economy of money, credit and financial investments. This economy is based strictly on information and new records are set in international financial markets every day.

More than ever, the growth and success of today's manufacturers depends on whether their customers prosper. In effect, the same is often true for customers themselves, whose ability to meet their own customers' demands rests upon reliable auditors to provide high-quality, competitively priced audits in a responsive manner. Today, major industrial companies rely on far fewer outside controls as a way to keep down costs, ensure replenishment of supply and maintain quality.

The supply chain into 2005

Increased supply chain implementation is today widely recognized as the stream of business processes through which materials, components and parts flow from source to end-consumer. Whether manufacturers supply goods to the public, to other manufacturers, to retailers or to wholesaler/distributors, customers of all sizes and types demand more value from the products and services they buy. As the sum of all their parts, products can only promote customer satisfaction and loyalty if their features, availability, serviceability, reliability and price meet that customer's expectations. It then becomes the job of each supply-chain participant to strive for and achieve these goals. Nevertheless, while preferred-supplier relationships provide companies with the opportunity to increase sales, the commitment can involve considerable investment to comply with customer requirements, such as electronic communication systems and inventory management techniques. There is also significant risk as companies expand their energies and resources on the success of fewer customers. Achieving and sustaining profitability is more critical than ever.

However, companies do not always exchange information on a constant basis. Only 44 per cent of companies frequently engage in performance measurement and comments with major customers. Such measures should include all of the major service levels, such as inventory turns, on-time deliveries, fill rates, quality and invoicing accuracy. Generally speaking, these reviews should occur at least quarterly to be effective.

Among the services that large companies, particularly those in the electronics sector, require from companies is inventory consignment. Additionally, some customers demand that suppliers implement vendor-managed inventory (VMI) systems. This advanced inventory management technique takes consigned inventories a step further by making the supplier responsible for gauging, tracking and even replenishing its customers' inventories, often at the production site.

All these findings suggest that, for manufacturers' customers, preferred-supplier relationships probably result in lower unit costs and some additional services. However, neither customers nor auditors appear to be leveraging these arrangements to the greatest extent. Companies are often caught in the crossfire between unceasing customer demands and the inability to control whether their suppliers' goods arrive correctly and on time. To be effective, companies must place the same demands for price, quality and delivery on their own suppliers to ensure prompt and cost-effective replenishment.

International expansion

Despite the many good reasons to expand internationally, 46 per cent of US-based manufacturing companies continue to see the USA as their primary market. The fact that nearly half of American manufacturers continue to rely on the domestic marketplace to fuel their growth is not surprising. Some industry sectors view the USA as a largely untapped market for their products. In addition, many companies have applied product improvements and operational efficiencies to recapture domestic customers previously lost to foreign competitors. By strengthening a domestic thrust, these services lack differentiation, fixed costs are high or the product is perishable, capacity is augmented in large increments, exit barriers are high, and/or the rivals are diverse in strategies, origins and personalities.

What is competitive advantage?

Competitive advantage is a company's ability to outperform its competitors. It can be achieved through low costs and product differentiation. A company is said to have achieved competitive advantage when its profit rate is higher than the average for its industry. The profit rate is based on return on sales (ROS) or return on assets (ROA). The most basic determinant of a company's profit rate is the gross profit margin. There are three reasons why a company's gross profit margin may be high: the unit price is higher, unit cost is lower, or it has both a higher price and a lower unit cost. When a company charges a premium price or differentiates its product, it is using generic business-level strategies. The building blocks of competitive advantage are efficiency, quality, innovation and customer responsiveness. These building blocks are generic in that they provide four basic ways to lower costs and achieve differentiation. Any firm can adopt these, no matter what industry it is in or what product or service it provides.

Efficiency is based on the cost of inputs required to produce a given output. Efficiency helps a company to attain a low-cost competitive advantage. Employee productivity can be the key to efficiency.

The impact of high product quality on competitive advantage is the creation of a brand name reputation, greater efficiency and, thus, lower costs. This enhanced reputation allows the firm to charge a higher price. At the same time, costs are down so profits are higher, thus there is a higher competitive advantage. Quality has become imperative for survival in most companies.

To achieve customer responsiveness, a company must deliver exactly what the customer wants when the customer wants it. A company must do everything it can to identify and satisfy customer needs. Steps taken to improve quality and efficiency are consistent with the goal of high customer responsiveness. There may be a need to customize goods and services to meet the demands of individual customers. Customer response time has become a big factor in increasing customer responsiveness. Other areas that aid in achieving higher customer responsiveness are superior design, service, and after-sales service and support. Distinctive competencies come from two sources: resources and capabilities. These sources are both tangible and intangible. To achieve distinctive competency, a company's resources must be both unique and valuable. A company's capabilities refer to its skills at coordinating resources and putting them to productive use. A company needs to develop strategies that build on existing resources and capabilities, as well as build additional resources and capabilities. The durability of a company's competitive advantage depends on three factors: the height of the barriers to imitation, the capability of its competitors and the dynamism of the industry. Barriers to imitation are the factors that make it difficult for a competitor to copy a company's distinctive competencies. The major determinant of the capability of a manufacturers can reap the rewards for as long as the potential exists without the distractions of cultivating brand new markets in unknown places. The maturing US economy is forcing all automotive and other consumer goods auditors to focus on improving quality, delivery performance, operations/cost effectiveness, new product/service development and product warranty costs, all at the same time. Some of the impacts of this expansion are discussed below.

The impact of technology

The need for well-educated auditors and control professionals is increasing, thanks to technology's potential to dramatically change organizations and business practices, reduce costs and create new opportunities. Technology has affected the business environment in three significant ways. First, it has increased our ability to capture, analyse and process tremendous amounts of data and information, as well as changing production and service processes. This has empowered the business decision-maker greatly. Second, technology has significantly affected the control process. While control objectives have remained constant, technology has altered the way in which systems should be controlled. Safeguarding assets, as a control objective, remains the same whether done manually or automated. Third, technology has affected the auditing profession in terms of the knowledge required to draw conclusions and the skills to perform an audit.

What does the external environment consist of? The firm's external environment consists of three main sectors: the remote environment, the industry environment and the operating environment. All of these environmental sectors affect the firm's operations on an international and domestic level.

The remote environment comprises five factors that are not influenced by a single firm. The main factors are economic, social, political, technological and ecological. The firm must consider these factors when working with the market.

The industry environment is made up of the entry barriers, supplier power, buyer power, substitute availability and competitive rivalry. These contending forces are of the greatest importance to the firm in strategy formulation.

In dealing with the threat of entry, there are six major barriers: economies of scale, product differentiation, capital requirements, cost disadvantages independent of size, access of distribution channels and government policies. These can be overcome or dealt with individually, but some companies are not able to handle them and thus fail.

A supplier becomes powerful when it purchases in large quantities, the products purchased are not differentiated, the product does not save the buyer money or the buyer poses a threat of backward integration. A buyer becomes powerful if it purchases in large volume, the product purchased is standard or undifferentiated, the product purchased represents a significant portion of the cost, it earns low profits or quality is not a factor. Substitute products become a problem if a company cannot differentiate the product or service in some way (i.e. cost or quality).

Jockeying for position by companies becomes intense when competitors are numerous, industry growth is slow, products or competitor is its prior strategic commitments. A dynamic industry changes rapidly, thus it has a high rate of product innovation. Companies fail for three related reasons: inertia, prior strategic commitments, and when a company becomes so dazzled by its early success that it believes more of the same effort is the only way to future success. To avoid failure, a company might focus on the building blocks of competitive advantage. A company must identify the best practice and adopt it. The best way to determine the best industrial practice is through re-evaluating its operations and applying best practices, implementing integrated enterprise resource planning (ERP)/material requirement planning (MRP) systems and regular industry benchmarking.

CHAPTER 2

An approach to profitability

The philosophy of a business turnaround includes six elements: (1) a common goal, (2) teamwork promotion, (3) a common language, (4) synergism, (5) comparison capability, and (6) desire for improvement. Each element is vital in achieving the end state of excellence in all we do.

In order to find out whether your company is on the right track, answer the questions below.

- Are we in the right line of business?

- Is our workforce the right size, and is it organized effectively for where our business is today?

- Is our financial/asset management appropriate for our business?

- Should we re-evaluate our products, site, employees or customer base?

- Is our current approach to sales/marketing effective for maximum profitability?

- Is our current approach to expense management sufficient to reduce costs and maximize productivity?

What is profitability?

Whether you're a senior executive in a Fortune 500 company or a mid-level manager in a smaller firm, your organization's bottom line can benefit from solutions for profitability. This profitability improvement programme enables companies to discover and eliminate waste, defects in their process or lack of quality. Profitability, as you know, is now widely regarded as the key to sustained competitive success in our global markets. You also know that in order to achieve profitability now, and in the future, quality has to be managed (in the same way that any important business function is managed). Solutions for profitability is a systematic way to unlock hidden productivity in your operations. It will require a disciplined approach that starts by defining your customer needs and then works backward through the process to measure, analyse, improve and control profitability.

It includes proven approaches such as balanced scorecards, key performance indicators and ROI to monitor value. However, it is the life-cycle approach of continuous measurement, analysis, planning and management action that ensures business benefits are realized. If a profitability programme is to succeed it must continually integrate process, organization, knowledge and technology. It must also provide links between strategic business goals and the business layers (e.g. business executive needs, business functions, business infrastructure services and support).

The basic steps include (1) completing a business analysis with representation from key areas of the company, (2) planning the actions required to implement the strategy, (3) identifying key performance measures and relationships between the outcomes and behaviours, and (4) establishing a measurement programme that continually measures the behaviour indicators and outcomes so that cause and effect relationships will be recognized and proactive management can take place.

What benefits should we expect from a successful profitability programme? The expectations are highest for companies that are experiencing high growth, increasing competition, lack of skilled resources and significant changes in organization, process and technology. Quite simply, a business profitability programme should facilitate success in these areas. A commitment to an ongoing profitability programme will yield results in the long term. These results include improved revenues, market share and profits. However, these results may take years to surface and the reason for the improvement could be occluded by other influences, making it difficult to point to the programme as the contributor. Other, more immediate, although less tangible, benefits not only address these issues but may be used as an early warning measure of what the bottom-line benefits will be. To ensure that these benefits are realized, the management team must support an ongoing programme of business profitability and see to it that the necessary enablers are in place.

Consider some possible uses and benefits of profitability improvement, shown in the box below.

Become proactive in profit contribution to the business.

Predict and pre-empt serious trends (lead indicators allow action before problems become unmanageable).

Reduce the risk involved with projects (pinpoint behaviours and prioritize investment based on business value).

Prove and improve the value of profitability (e.g. revenue, market share, growth, change adaptability, customer satisfaction, cost of business/service, productivity, efficiency, quality, learning, skills inventory).

Justify projects and budgets.

Make better use of limited skills and resources.

Benchmark internal projects (measure the 'before and after' results of activities).

Benchmark your company against competitors and 'industry best' programmes.

Visualize common goals and how each group contributes to achieving them.

Create a stakeholder culture at a grass-roots level.

Make decisions quickly and confidently.

Which values are we trying to measure and improve?

Traditionally, measures of success have been economic, like revenue or market share. The problem with using these metrics to indicate value is that they fail to measure the less tangible benefits and only reflect a delayed snapshot of business performance, thus making it too late to avoid a problem once it has been detected. This is true with more and more industries where the accelerating rate of change requires even quicker decision-making and reactions. Managing a business proactively and effectively today requires that we balance the lagging indicator measurements with other measures that forecast economic results through early warnings. To this end, recent measures have become recognized as leading indicators (early warnings) of whether a company will achieve its business goals. A well documented example includes customer satisfaction as a leading indicator of a company's future market share and revenue. However, there are other internal processes and values that drive success as well. Measuring these (e.g. staff training, internal processes, service metrics, etc.) will provide early warnings and a more accurate measure of the internal business or contribution. Optionally, these internal metrics may be used to measure and manage the operational aspects of the specific internal business or function. This helps managers to forecast, diagnose and optimize their operation and the contribution it makes to the business.

Once we have identified the business goals, we need to identify the behaviours within the areas that are identified as contributors to business benefits. Correctly mapping the behaviours back to strategic goals is crucial and requires not only a good understanding of each function or process but also of the interaction between them. Only through this mapping can we define lead indicators that forecast a company's success, thereby allowing us to be proactive in managing to achieve the business goals. Many of these lead indicators (behaviour metrics) are applied within the standardized high-level categories of capability, customer satisfaction, performance, learning/ knowledge, process, quality and contributing factors.

Many of these measures are already in use at both layers but may not be mapped back to business benefits or consolidated in a way that makes trends and relationships easy to detect. A measurement programme is a critical component of the overall profitability programme and while many existing metrics are available, the degree to which they are suitable for any one implementation is dependent on many factors.

How do we implement a profitability programme?

In order to succeed with profitability, we must consider implementation from the outset. Technical implementation may be the least of our concerns if we consider that many of the success drivers are subtle and easily overlooked. Dealing with the dynamics that exist at various levels within an organization's value chain is an imperative.

We need to consider the following issues:

- Awareness and commitment are crucial at all participating levels within the organization, especially at the senior executive level.

- Involving stakeholders in early workshops broadens the collective experience and perspective and is the first step toward changing attitudes and behaviours to help to achieve business objectives.

- An automated and integrated programme that is embedded in existing or specialized technologies improves the chance of continuous profitability.

- We must measure and map correctly and dynamically from a business value perspective.

- Profitability is not an add-on, but is simply a measurement of the existing processes and systems already in place. The measures are the system.

- Critical to the success of the profitability measurement programme is the need for a simple solution that will take hold at a grass-roots level – one that is easy to adapt for each business or function. Figure 2.1 shows a basic business process flow for core business competencies.

Here is a six-step method to achieve profitability.

The six steps to profitability

1. Define the problem

- What are we trying to accomplish (e.g. trying to decide how much output to produce)?

- In what context (e.g. managers in the private sector vs. in the public sector)?

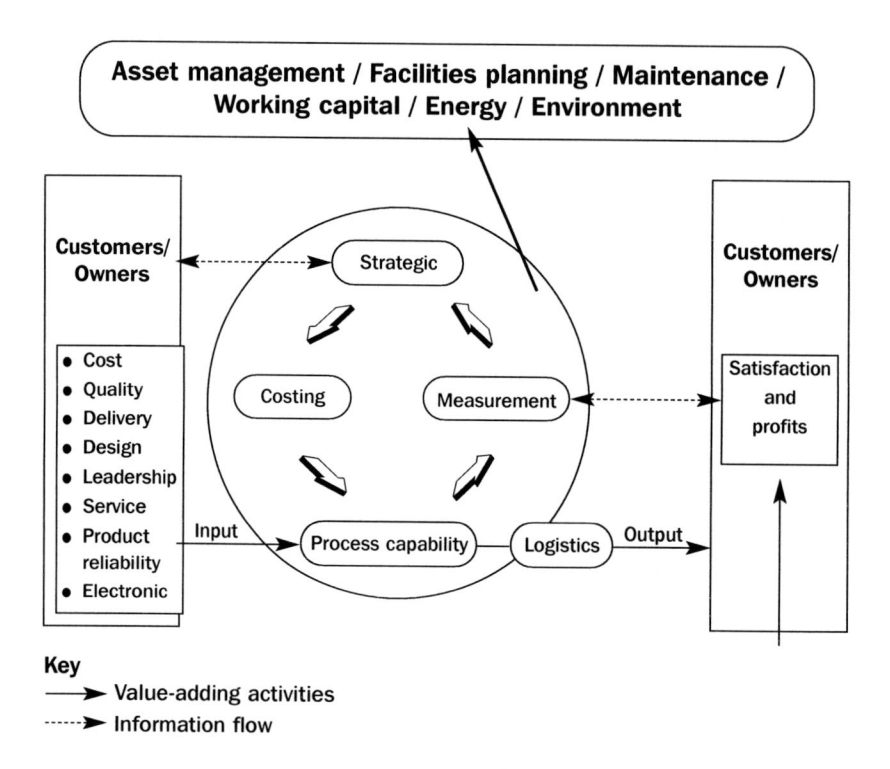

Figure 2.1 Strategic profit approach.

2. Determine the objective

- What is our overall goal (e.g. to maximize profit)?

- What is our operational goal (e.g. we face uncertainty about key variables)?

3. Explore the alternatives

- What variables can we control?

- What are our constraints (e.g. we can only retool so quickly)?

4. *Predict the consequences*

- What is our model?

5. *Make a choice*

- We seek ways to make optimal decisions.

6. *Perform sensitivity analysis*

- What happens if our assumptions are wrong?

Comparison capability

By providing variance for process complexity, you can compare similar processes to determine overall performance and improvement opportunities.

Desire for improvement

Current metrics are reactive in nature. When we don't meet a desired standard, we make changes to the process or metric to achieve the standard. The solutions for profitability concept is proactive in nature by communicating current performance, allowing moving goals to be established for continuous improvement. Figure 2.2 illustrates the strategic profit approach that encompasses both profitability and customer satisfaction.

Marketing
Design
MRP-ERP
Energy
Machining
Facilities
Tooling
Processes
Maintenance
Distribution
Shipping
Logistics

Strategic

Cash flow

Human resources

Accounting

Business plan

Finance

Production

Protection of environment

Inventory

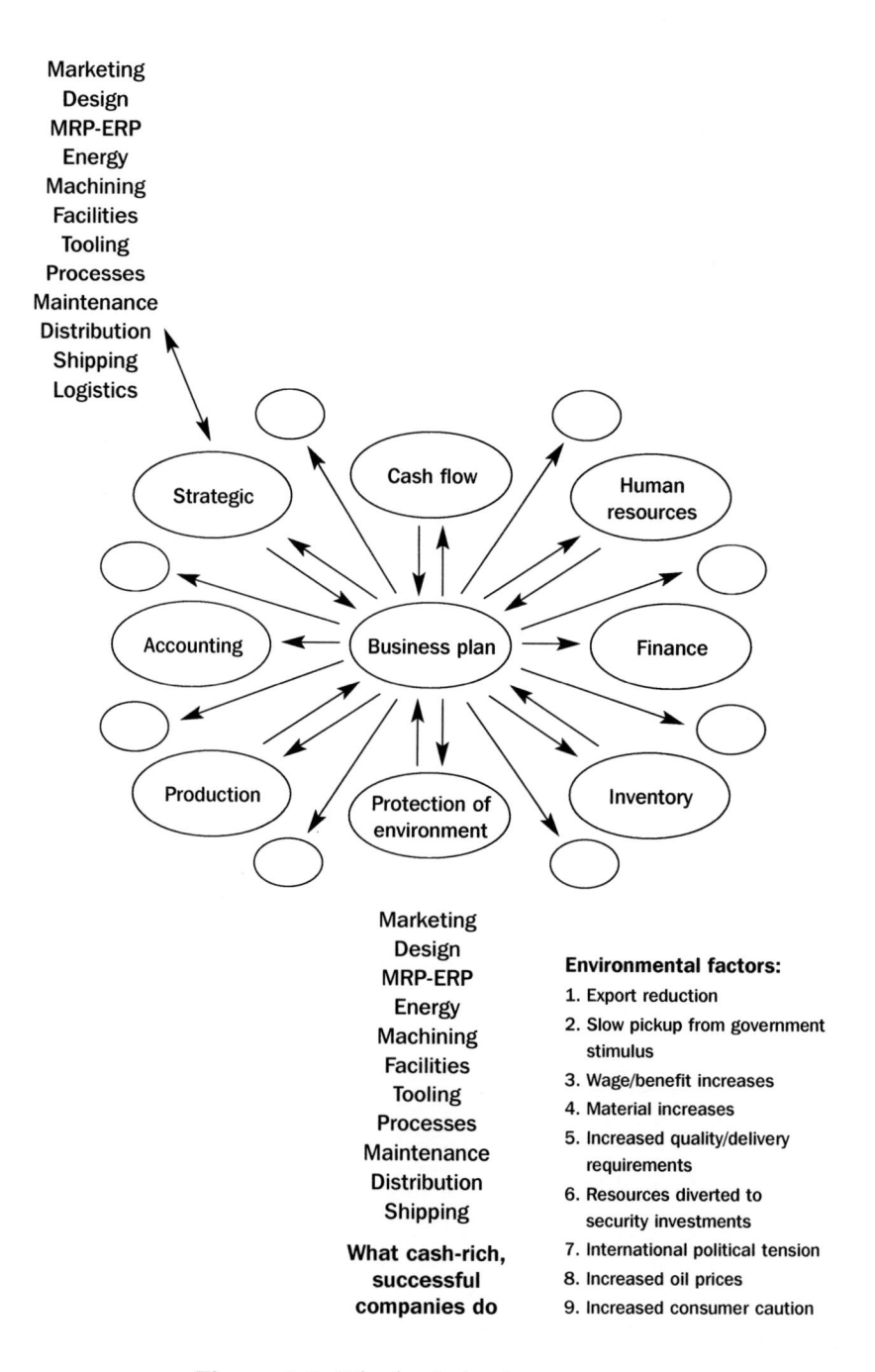

Marketing
Design
MRP-ERP
Energy
Machining
Facilities
Tooling
Processes
Maintenance
Distribution
Shipping

What cash-rich, successful companies do

Environmental factors:
1. Export reduction
2. Slow pickup from government stimulus
3. Wage/benefit increases
4. Material increases
5. Increased quality/delivery requirements
6. Resources diverted to security investments
7. International political tension
8. Increased oil prices
9. Increased consumer caution

Figure 2.2 The basic business process.

Core management components

The business analysis and planning process involves management putting down on paper how the company currently performs and where it wants to go. It is the roadmap for the company's future. The analysis is made up of all the general business functions that define a successful business and illustrate where the company needs to focus its attention. Planning the future by improving performance and objectives will significantly increase your chances of meeting business objectives. Use the following as a guide.

1. **Business management**
(a) Statement of the firm's mission, vision, goals and objectives.
(b) Description of the firm's ownership structure.
(c) Organization chart identifying positions and names of all professionals, technicians and administrative personnel.
(d) Job descriptions of key personnel.
(e) Outline indicating the scope of the firm's services.
(f) Policy and procedure for strategic planning and tactical implementation.

2. **Facilities and technical resources**
(a) Standards for space and furniture allocation.
(b) Inventory of major laboratory equipment, field instrumentation, safety equipment, computers and other available facilities or resources.
(c) Statement of procedures and description of facilities for handling and storing hazardous materials, contaminated samples and specialized equipment used in geo-environmental operations.

3. Human resources management

(a) Procedures for monitoring laws and regulations that affect the firm's practices.
(b) Equal opportunity/affirmative action plans.
(c) Substance abuse screening/testing policies.
(d) Background check policies and procedures.
(e) Description of recruitment procedures.
(f) Personnel manuals and procedures.
(g) Medical monitoring programme.
(h) Health and safety programme.
(i) Performance review procedures.
(j) Employee advancement policies.
(k) CVs of professional and technical personnel.
(l) Management information systems for personnel experience records.
(m) Description of retention strategies.
(n) Exit interview guidelines.

4. Professional development

(a) Professional development and continuing education policies.
(b) Descriptions of employee training programmes.
(c) Seminar and professional organization attendance policies.
(d) Registration/certification policies.

5. Project management

(a) Standard contract(s).
(b) Policy for including construction-phase services in the scope of service.
(c) Procedures for assigning personnel to projects.

(d) Communication policies and procedures.

(e) Procedures for maintaining client confidentiality.

(f) Communication recording systems; documentation policies.

(g) Systems for storage and retrieval of the firm's current and prior records.

(h) Record retention/purging policies.

(i) Job cost recording procedures.

(j) Guidelines for monitoring project progress and completion, including billing and financial tracking.

(k) Procedures for identifying individuals who performed and/or reviewed specific work.

(l) Warning systems to alert personnel to signs of trouble.

(m) Overrun reviews and procedures.

(n) Quality assurance (QA)/quality control (QC) procedures for review of technical correspondence and reports.

6. Financial management

(a) Procedure for budget and business plan development.

(b) Policy for regular preparation of financial statements.

(c) Procedure for monitoring backlog of work.

(d) Billing procedures.

(e) Collection procedures.

(f) Procedures for the timely distribution of a project's financial data.

(g) Procedures for storage and retrieval of financial records.

7. Marketing and business development

(a) Statement of qualifications.

(b) Quality assurance review procedures for marketing publications.

(c) Brochures and/or other marketing materials (including website, news releases, etc.).

(d) Guidelines for responding to requests for proposals.

(e) Procedures for screening potential clients and projects before accepting them.

(f) Identification of persons authorized to commit the firm contractually on projects.

(g) Marketing plan.

8. **Electronic resources**

(a) Policies for acquisition and maintenance of hardware and software.

(b) Established monitoring procedures for software licensing compliance.

(c) Organizational definition of responsibility and authority for planning, implementing and maintaining the firm's information systems infrastructure.

(d) Written policies for maintenance of electronic data files, back-up procedure, system security and staff use, and management surveillance of facilities for appropriate use for company business.

(e) Guidelines for business and personal uses of company e-mail and Internet services.

(f) Software inventory.

CHAPTER 3

Self-assessment

Recently I conducted a need assessment with my manufacturing and distribution client base (60 small to mid-sized companies in most industries) and found a significant change in business needs and requirements was needed in order for the businesses to survive in the future. The top three issues facing small to mid-sized companies reflect the strategies they are pursuing to survive and thrive in today's business environment. The top three issues are: (1) adapting quickly to market changes (69 per cent); (2) developing intimate customer relationships (68 per cent); and (3) differentiating the company's unique value in the marketplace (67 per cent).

Also of significant importance are issues of attracting and retaining talent, developing creative and valuable strategic alliances, and developing strategies for getting more value from information technology investments. This data reflects interviews with 404 business owners across four industry groups: technology, community banks, consumer and industrial products, and other companies with annual revenues between $5 million and $500 million (between

$100 million and $2 billion in assets for community banks). These interviews were conducted between 11 March and 2 April 2002.

Companies are advised to watch out for waste that sometimes comes along with an improving business climate. Lean growth is the order of the day. Manufacturers need to be cautious about growing too quickly without a strong business strategy in place. While it appears that the economy is slowly turning around, companies should use this time to understand their value stream. During a growth period, manufacturers need to have a good knowledge of their manufacturing and distribution capacity; it pays to be judicious.

What you have to know and do

Know your capacity

In order to expand smartly, you need to have a good understanding of your manufacturing and distribution capacity. You can do this by understanding your value stream and uncovering any bottlenecks in your supply chain. The capacity constraint could be a specific work centre, support process or facility constraint.

Define your core competencies

Now is a good time to redefine your core competencies and decide what direction your company should move in. Explore new products and technologies to see if they make sense for your company. Use this time to get rid of obsolete technologies and products that aren't bringing value to your organization or customers.

Evaluate your suppliers

In reviewing your value stream, you may find that your suppliers are the bottleneck. Long lead times could put you behind the delivery curve at your company or cause you to carry excess inventory. By understanding where problems exist in the supply chain, manufacturers can work with those suppliers that serve your organization best, seek solutions to ease the jam, or identify new suppliers. This will require a collaborative relationship with the suppliers to develop a 'win–win' strategy.

Be choosy about adding capacity

As the economy recovers, demand will increase and there may be a real need to add capacity, not just in the manufacturing process, but in key support areas as well. It is essential to have a good awareness of your capacity and core competencies before adding capacity. In some cases, it may make sense to outsource instead of adding to your overheads.

Manage payrolls smartly

Finding the right number of employees is vital to the future success of your company. Perform a capacity or staffing model based on accurate value streams to determine what your staffing levels should be at different levels of demand. Underhiring can be just as

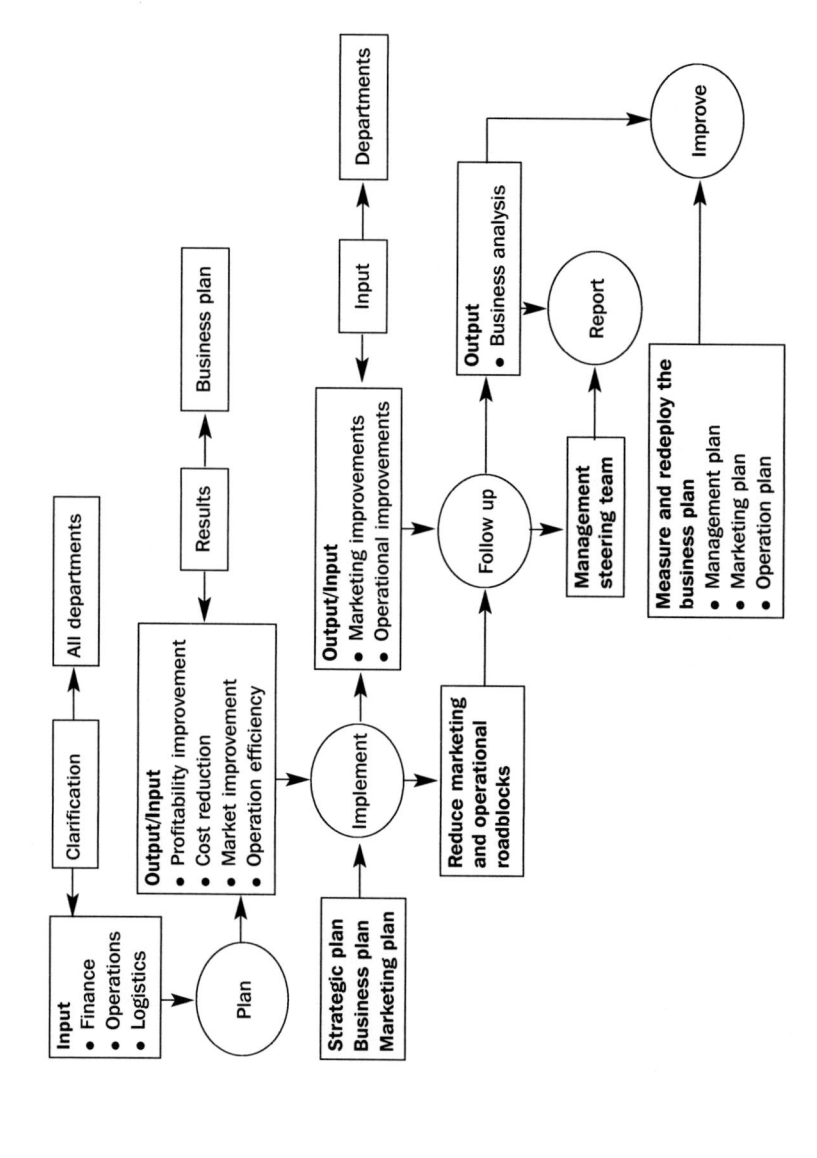

Figure 3.1 The profitability improvement process.

dangerous to a company's long-term growth as overhiring. Figure 3.1 demonstrates a comprehensive profitability improvement process.

Now take the time to do a quick self-assessment on your company using the following questionnaire.

Indicators of a strong business

In a healthy and financially sound business, strategic, financial and operational functions are in balance. In many cases, a company cannot work on all areas at once. The manager must decide which area to concentrate on, based on past practices and the needs of the business. Regular use of the audit instrument below can help make the business manager more efficient:

Mission statements

- The company has a clearly defined mission.
- There is a written mission statement.
- The company is carrying out its mission.
- The mission statement is modified when necessary.
- Employees understand and share in the mission.

Increasing competitive performance

- The company has a written sales plan.
- A market niche has been identified.
- New product lines are developed when appropriate.
- Targeted customers are being reached.
- Sales are increasing.

Budgets and pricing structures

- The company has an annual budget.
- The budget is used as a flexible guide.
- The budget is used as a control device.
- Actual expenditures are compared against budgeted expenditures.
- Corrective action is taken when expenses are over budget.
- The owner prepares the budget.
- The budget is realistic.
- The company has a pricing policy.
- Products or services are competitively priced.
- The business provides volume discounts.
- Prices are increased when warranted.
- There is a relationship between pricing changes and sales volume.
- New prices are placed on last-in goods when the price on old stock is changed.

Monitoring employees

- Employees know what is expected of them.
- Each employee has only one supervisor.
- Supervisors have authority commensurate with their responsibility.
- Employees volunteer critical information to their supervisor.
- Employees are using their skills on the job.
- Employees feel adequately trained.
- Each employee has a job description.

- Employees can accurately describe what they do.
- Employees do what is expected of them.
- Workload is distributed equitably.
- Employees receive feedback on their performance.
- Employees are rewarded for good performance.
- Employees are familiar with company policies.
- There is a concise policy manual.
- Preventive discipline is used when appropriate.
- Employees are informed when performance is below standard.
- Non-excused absences are dealt with immediately.
- Theft prevention measures are in place.
- Regular employee meetings are conducted.
- Employees' ideas are solicited at meetings.
- An agenda is given to employees prior to meetings.

Suppliers

- The company has a good relationship with suppliers.
- A well-documented plan addresses how to deal with suppliers.
- Inventory delivery times are specified.
- Levels of quality of materials and service are specified.
- Payment terms are documented.
- Contingency plans are provided.
- Regular contact is made with suppliers.

Inventory

- The company provides for good inventory control.
- The company has an inventory control formula to provide for optimum inventory levels.
- The company has a policy on securing inventory in a timely fashion.
- The company conducts incoming inventory inspections.
- The company has a written policy on incoming inspection.
- Incoming inspection is being performed.
- Incoming inspection levels of quality are documented.
- The company has alternative sources of raw materials.
- Two or more suppliers are identified for each product needed.
- The majority of raw material requirements is divided equally between two major suppliers with a third source receiving lesser but consistent orders.

Equipment and maintenance

- The company has a routine maintenance programme.
- A routine maintenance programme is documented and communicated to all maintenance personnel.
- Every major piece of equipment has a maintenance log positioned in an obvious place.
- Preventive maintenance is a regular occurrence.
- The company has a formal operator training programme.
- The company has a written operator training manual.

Training/safety measures

- A progressive training process is in place.
- Experienced operators are available to answer questions from trainees.
- Constructive feedback on training progress is provided in a non-intimidating fashion.
- The company meets Occupational Safety and Health Administration (OSHA) standards.
- The company is aware of OSHA standards pertaining to the business.
- The company conducts regular meetings with employees concerning OSHA standards.
- All safety records and lost-time accidents are documented.
- The company has a well-documented processing procedure.
- A scheduling process enables orders to be grouped for efficient processing.
- A scheduling chart allowing instantaneous recognition of production status is in an obvious place.
- Sub-assemblies are manufactured in sufficient quantities on a timely basis.
- Finished stock is safely transported to a clean and dry area.
- Adequate controls are provided to preclude excessive inventory buildups that could result in finished stock spoilage or obsolescence.
- The company has an environmental awareness policy.
- A policy pertaining to the disposition of hazardous waste materials is fully documented and communicated to all pertinent parties.

- Attempts are made to stay current with all existing regulations pertaining to the environment.

Retaining organizational focus

- Regular meetings are conducted to determine better methods of dealing with by-products.
- The company attempts to stay current with technological advances.
- Company representatives attend trade shows on a regular basis.
- The company subscribes to trade publications.
- A formal employee suggestion programme is in place.
- The company conducts regular technology advancement brainstorming sessions involving its employees.
- The company is involved in the community's extended learning programmes.
- The owner knows exactly what the business is.
- The owner knows exactly who the customer is.
- Potential customers know about the business.
- Its location is appropriate for the business.
- The market is clearly defined.
- The owner knows competitors and their location.
- The owner knows how his prices compare with the competition's.
- The owner knows how the competition is regarded.
- Census data are used for strategic marketing.
- The owner knows the sales patterns.
- The owner and employees focus on customer needs.

- The owner and employees treat customers courteously.
- Customers' concerns, complaints and suggestions are listened to carefully.
- Customers are provided with quick, reliable service.
- Customers consider the owner knowledgeable.
- Appropriate housekeeping procedures for the business are followed.
- The owner is aware of customer needs.
- Feedback is requested from customers.

Improving profitability

- Sales receipts are monitored.
- Sales receipts are compared to those from previous years.
- Seasonal variations are taken into account.
- The company needs to increase sales volume.
- There is a sales plan in effect.
- Sales goals are being met.
- Effective sales presentations are being made to potential customers.
- Names of prospects are kept in a follow-up file.
- Sales are closed effectively.
- The owner has an advertising and promotion plan.
- The owner has an advertising budget.
- The owner advertises monthly.
- The owner advertises weekly.
- The owner has a promotional calendar.
- The owner uses effective advertising and promotion.

- The owner advertises in the Yellow Pages.
- The owner uses newspapers and shoppers.
- The owner uses radio and television advertising.
- The owner obtains no-cost or low-cost media coverage.
- The owner uses effective merchandising techniques.
- The owner relates display space to sales potential.
- The owner uses vendor promotional aids.
- The owner knows traffic-flow patterns of customers.
- The owner evaluates advertising and promotional efforts.
- The owner determines if sales increase with advertising.
- The owner ascertains if sales increase after special promotions.
- The owner finds out whether advertising is reaching intended market.

General book-keeping and accounting practices

- The company has a book-keeping system; single entry; double entry.
- The company prepares its own books.
- The company prepares its own financial statements.
- The company pays for book-keeping services.
- The company understands financial statements.
- The company has compared the cost of a book-keeper with that of a CPA.
- The company reconciles bank statements monthly.
- The company keeps income and expenses statements accurate and prepares statements monthly.
- The company understands the purpose of financial statements.

- The company compares several monthly statements for trends.
- The company compares statements against industry averages.
- The company knows current financial status of business.
- The company makes monthly deposits for business withholding and social security taxes.
- The company makes deposits on time to avoid penalties.
- The company has a credit policy.
- The company accesses late payment fees from customers.
- The company writes off bad debts.
- The company has a good collection policy.
- The company has a series of increasingly pointed letters to collect from late customers.
- The company has Visa, Mastercard or other credit.
- The company emphasizes cash discounts.
- The company files all tax returns in a timely manner.
- The company considers tax implications of purchasing new equipment early.
- The company considers buy versus lease possibilities.
- The company considers possible advantages/disadvantages of incorporation/sub-chapters.
- The company does not pay tax penalties (business, state and sales).
- The company has adequate cash flow.
- Pre-numbered cash receipts are monitored and accounted for.
- Cheques are deposited properly each day.
- Customer invoicing is done promptly (within two working days).
- Collections are received within 60 days.

- Accounts payable take advantage of cash discounts.
- Disbursements are made by pre-numbered cheque.

Managing risk

- Payrolls are met without problems.
- Money is set aside for expansion, emergencies and opportune purchases.
- Short-term financing is used when needed.
- A line of credit is established with a bank.
- The company understands the role of financial planning in today's highly competitive lending markets.
- The owner's personal CV is prepared and current.
- Personal financial statements have been prepared.
- The business has a written business plan.
- Source and use of funds statements exist for the past two years, with a business plan for the next two years.
- An accurate balance sheet exists for the past two years and includes a business plan for the next two years.
- The owner has a good working relationship with a banker.
- There is a strong debt-to-equity ratio.

Case study 3.1 ABC Manufacturing

They know what their competitors do, they know what their customers think, they know what technology has to offer, and they know what their capabilities are.

History

In the beginning, ABC Manufacturing made customized equipment for producing curved printing plates, produced tools and dies, and did contract machining. ABC Manufacturing's management style and the quality of their work gained them a steady stream of customers. Within a year, the company became incorporated as ABC Engineering, Inc. Within two years, the company had moved to a new location and had 15 employees.

Over the next ten years, ABC continued to manufacture custom-designed machines, including photo register equipment used in the printing industry and tape applying machines for 3M. ABC also continued to provide contract precision machining services. As the company grew, ABC Engineering, Inc. didn't forget those who had helped make it a success. In 1956, the CEO instituted the company's first profit-sharing plan. In 1962, ABC moved again; this time to a 27,000 sq. ft. facility. To take advantage of the space, ABC added $100,000 worth of new equipment. At this point, it employed 55 people. By the end of the year, this had jumped to 75 and company sales exceeded $1 million.

The years 1960 to 1980 marked a period of rapid expansion. In 1963, the company developed the fixtures that support the appliance during the injection of foam insulation in refrigerators and freezers. It also developed machines to assemble typewriter-ribbon cassettes, place magnetic tape on ledger cards, package carbon paper, and plate chain. In response to the growth, the company continued expanding – first to 44,000 sq. ft, then to 73,000 sq. ft. In 1970, the company purchased 67 acres near Big Lake, Minnesota. Eventually, it built two plants on the property.

Early on, ABC had decided against borrowing to finance capital equipment. Instead, it used internal funding resources to acquire new machines and additional capabilities. The philosophy remains. Even today, the company finances virtually all its capital equipment using inside sources. Outside financing is occasionally used to purchase property and erect buildings.

By 1976, ABC had reached $8 million in annual sales. To boost revenues, it set up a national sales force. Within six years, revenues exceeded $26 million. Once again, the company added equipment and plant space, this time by purchasing a plant for its automation systems activities. In the late 1980s, the company continued to invest in equipment and people, often committing to a promising technology, then later finding the business to support it. By 1989, sales exceeded $60 million.

Today, ABC Engineering, Inc. has more than 475 employees and annual revenues of approximately $90 million. Its customers include computer companies, car manufacturers, the aerospace/aircraft/defence/space industry and others. Although the company is one of the largest job shops in the USA, it maintains the same philosophy that ABC Manufacturing began.

Operating philosophy

ABC's overall corporate goal is to be the best in its field. The company also emphasizes customer satisfaction, employee satisfaction, profitability and growth. To achieve these goals, ABC has adopted several operating principles. These include:

1. *Maintaining a small plant atmosphere*. ABC feels that good communication is important for profitable growth. To that end, the company

guidelines state that the optimum desired employment at any one plant is 200 people and, to avoid excessive dependence and to limit risk, the guidelines also limit the percentage of resources it will dedicate to one customer and the amount of business it will take in any one industry.

According to ABC's management, this philosophy has a number of advantages. It helps management to maintain close working relationships with their customers as well as their employees. It encourages the diversification of jobs and customers. It allows ABC to maintain a nurturing environment. It gives employees the opportunity for recognition based on their contributions, and this in turn leads to high morale. It also allows ABC to avoid dramatic declines that come from depending too much on one company or industry sector.

In addition, keeping the plant small enables customers to know everyone involved in their job. For their part, the employees feel a sense of ownership. Recently, a prospective customer visited one of ABC's plants unannounced and met with the group supervisor and machine operator, as management was otherwise engaged. The operator showed the customer how he was going to approach the project and showed his thought preparation with a software package that displayed the tool path he had worked out. The prospective customer became a customer, impressed that ABC's operators knew exactly what they were going to do from a technical perspective during the estimation and proposal stage.

When a plant grows too large, ABC will spin off one of its capabilities into an independent operating unit. This helps maintain an entrepreneurial atmosphere, sense of excitement and team spirit within the company. Employees want to know when they are going to split off and become their own plant or division.

2. *Encouraging employee loyalty*. The company's overriding philosophy is: 'We all succeed or fail together.'

ABC tries to empower everyone. For example, when the company was deciding whether to establish high-velocity machining capability, it formed a committee of six people, four of whom were machinists, to make the recommendation. The committee searched the world for the best equipment available, eventually visiting machine manufacturers in France and Germany and talking to their customers. The committee returned with a recommendation that was presented to all divisional employees by the machinists on the committee.

To ensure availability of the highest skilled machinists and encourage the learning environment, ABC invests as much as $100,000 in apprenticeship and training programmes for new employees. The company also provides tuition for every employee in any field as long as it is related to some function at the company.

ABC is a non-union shop that believes in paying its employees a competitive wage. ABC competes for highly skilled people where journeyman machinists can earn $50,000 per year or more. In addition, the company maintains a profit-sharing programme based on corporate profitability.

The company values its employees as family and will reduce hours to avoid layoffs. It conducts a yearly attitude survey, and gives employees as much responsibility as possible. For example, machine operators in one division are also responsible for purchasing, quality control and machine maintenance. In essence, they are in charge of their own performance and their own success. To that end, ABC employees are often involved in the hiring process. Typically, those people who will work with a potential employee will interview and help make the hiring decision.

For their part, employees are encouraged to suggest improvements and develop solutions to customer problems or demands, instead of waiting for solutions to come from management. They are also expected to return the company's loyalty through their performance on the job, in keeping with the corporate goal to be the best in its field.

3. *Practising the art of informed risk*. ABC encourages its employees to make decisions based on knowledge. Mistakes and even losses are accepted as part of the learning curve.

   The company invests heavily and constantly in new technologies and is recognized by both competitors and customers for its leadership in this area. Typically, the company will commit millions of dollars to a new technology or piece of equipment, and to the learning curve, before taking the new capability to market.

   Recently a five-axis machine was purchased without any exhibited interest from customers to influence the decision. ABC had been using three-axis capability for some jobs that could use a five-axis machine effectively, and they perceived a potential market for five-axis machine application. After learning and experience with the new equipment had developed knowledge and skills, the company promoted the capability to current and potential customers. This led to the new tooling design and build segment of its business. In another example, a particular part needed more cost-effective production. Both the customer and ABC looked for ways to reduce or eliminate assembly time and the need for assembly equipment. ABC spent a year and half exploring process technology alternatives. The knowledge the company gained not only helped them address the customer's needs but served to increase machining speeds in applications throughout the company.

Their eye is always on the long term. When learning is combined with perceived potential, ABC will subsidize a loss. ABC's automation division was carried through several years of money-losing operation when conditions changed that removed a traditional market. Belief in the people and the perception of long-term value, coupled with hard-working attempts at different approaches, has paid off as the plant has returned to profitability.

Lines of business

The general machining division has two plants. Plant 10 produces low-quantity or small-lot runs in a 111,000 sq. ft. facility that incorporates design/build of tooling, fixturing and fabrication, and utilizes five-axis machining and other advanced equipment to produce parts up to 10 tons and 10 feet. Plant 40 is a 153,000 sq. ft. facility that produces low volumes and large parts (up to 75 tons and 100 feet) and features a 100 ft. CNC 7-inch milling and boring machine and a five-axis mill with 63 feet of travel.

The repetitive batch machining division is housed in Plant 20, a 49,000 sq. ft. facility dedicated to the repetitive batch manufacturing of medium-sized parts and assemblies in medium volumes. It specializes in parts that can fit within a two-foot cube and features machining centres and flexible manufacturing systems with operating speeds up to 40,000 RPM.

The production machining division is housed in the 60,000 sq. ft. plant 30 facility. It features a focused-factory cell concept that does a lot of dedicated outsourcing and can produce high volumes of precision machined parts. It is particularly suited to work in the two-foot cube and under category, with special capabilities for miniature precision machined parts typically under one cubic inch in size. The plant also features a class 100 clean room.

The automation division is in the 87,000 sq. ft. plant 50 and houses engineering and design services for developing one-of-a-kind factory automation equipment and systems. The facility contains design, fabrication, parts machining, assembly and testing capabilities.

Conclusion

ABC showed an initial concern that this case study would paint them as too accomplished, taking the edge off their continued quest. Later, when reviewing our maturity assessments, the opposite reaction occurred: some of the management team felt that they were not performing as well as they should be. We suggested that they were so far ahead of anyone else that this didn't matter and that the whole area of change proficiency has no history yet. We also observed that things were moving so fast that our snapshot of ABC's status was already out of date. In the eight-month project effort we witnessed information technology strategy come a long way in the direction of greater change proficiency maturity, we witnessed a high-velocity machining experiment turn into a new line of business, and we witnessed one division that had lost important business come back with a vengeance.

CHAPTER 4

Business turnaround

Let's hope your organization never has serious problems. However, the first step if this does happen is to recognize the early warning signs of financial distress. They include:

1. escalating inventory levels

2. relatively low cash balances

3. some payables being paid 15 days late

4. falling sales margins

5. production becoming inefficient and requiring improvement

6. your bank calling and asking for recent financials and additional information.

If you fail to take corrective action at this stage, then serious problems will occur, which will lead to other, more serious, problems: cash balances may be dangerously low; vendor payments get later; you can barely make payroll; layoffs start; employee morale falls; some of the better people will resign; creditors and banks will request meetings; you can't find and keep good employees; cash flow is going down the drain; new competition is eating up your markets; you can't beat your competition on price; customer demands are escalating; you can't serve the customers you've got. However, this spiral can be stopped. Read on to learn how.

Companies susceptible to trouble

Given the market forces of capitalism, all businesses are as vulnerable to trouble as they are to the lure of success. We live in a world of rapidly changing technologies. Even with these changes, a business that is managed properly will continue to prosper. However, some industries are more susceptible to trouble than others, due to various factors and characteristics.

The fortunes of companies in cyclical industries often depend upon forces outside their control such as commodity prices or weather conditions. Those most likely to withstand the effects of these forces are the ones that learn to adapt. They either sufficiently diversify without losing sight of their primary business or learn to control fixed costs in unstable conditions. The ability to adapt is key.

Companies in newly deregulated industries face having to learn to survive in a competitive environment without the legal protection they previously enjoyed. Deregulation is generally accompanied by an anticipated shakeout of the weakest businesses as competitive forces take hold in the marketplace.

As the USA has evolved from a primarily manufacturing-driven economy to an economy increasingly driven by service-oriented industries, management must recognize that its most irreplaceable assets are employees. Managing human resources is more important than ever. Companies lacking a proprietary product are subject to attack from every direction. Examples of these companies are retail businesses and non-licensed service sector businesses. They face low entry barriers both with respect to capital and expertise and a multitude of competitors.

Many companies and start-ups are single-product, single-customer companies. In order to succeed, these companies must usually develop new products or diversify to compete and satisfy customers. Few are able to maintain their start-up success, but instead struggle to compete with existing competition and new market entrants. Reaching maturity takes years, during which the company is vulnerable. Rapidly growing companies are often driven by business executive zeal and by an overwhelming emphasis on sales growth. Often, inadequate attention is paid to the effects of growth on the balance sheet. With huge sales increases and significant investments in R&D, these companies suddenly find themselves in a situation where the balance sheet simply cannot support their growth.

Highly leveraged companies have so many factors that must converge to be successful that they are often most susceptible to the external uncontrollable causes of business failure, such as interest rate fluctuations or an increase in raw material costs. Closely held businesses and family-owned businesses, by their nature, select leadership based not upon managerial talent but by virtue of family or close personal relationships with the shareholders. More than in other businesses, owner/managers link their personal psyche to that of their business. To owner/managers, business failure is often perceived as personal failure. Owner/managers often believe that they are irreplaceable or are afraid to admit that they are not. They want to maintain control and, consequently, they fail to either develop a management team or a plan for transition of management. These owner/managers are reluctant to acknowledge the early warning signs of failure and are also apt to ignore them.

Perhaps declining industries face the most difficult task of all. Declining industries are those in which total industry-wide unit shipments are declining. Maintaining market share involves shrinking. Maintaining volume involves increasing market share (i.e. taking business from competitors). Management that refuse to admit that their industry is declining or bet their future on the industry recovering are the most prone to failure.

Approximately 70 per cent of business executives and start-ups fail within two years. Business executives do not necessarily come from managerial backgrounds. They have visions of what the future will look like; their modus operandi is to capitalize on their head start as a way to convert their vision to a profitable reality. The same skills that keep a business executive focused on an idea, regardless of obstacles, can make him oblivious to the competition on his heels or to new changes in the market. Ultimately, the market does catch up, forcing the business executive to compete in a mature industry rather than in an emerging industry. As business executives survive the transition to professional management and new technologies gain strength in the economy, emerging industries are born.

Before you hire a turnaround expert, ask yourself these questions. Have business issues been isolated from personal issues? Or is the primary goal of hiring a turnaround specialist to protect the owner from personal guarantees and preserve personally owned assets? Are management (business sponsors) willing to admit that business problems are, in all likelihood, the result of mismanagement? Are they willing to become, if necessary, students rather than teachers or followers rather than leaders? If asked to give up control of the business, are management (business sponsors and business management) willing to do so? Are they willing to face their own shortcomings and to face facts that may reflect badly on their ability? Can management learn to function in a highly controlled environment, subject to being monitored by outsiders? Are they willing to accept the failure of the business, since some businesses are simply not savable? Are they willing to agree to a turnaround specialist's engagement if the only realistic expectation is to maximize liquidation value even if the ultimate result is the failure of the business? Are they willing to sell control and become both a minority shareholder and an employee of a new board of directors, if necessary, to attract the capital to preserve the company? Are management, in the case of smaller businesses particularly, willing to face the stigma of bankruptcy?

When a business turnaround may work

The following are some key points to consider in relation to turnarounds:

1. Take 24 hours to redefine your company's goals. Write these down. A turnaround is wasted effort if you do not know where you are going.

2. Assess, very quickly, your company's current status. This should only take a few days or a week or two. Put everything on the table: the things you prefer not to look at can cause you to go under.

3. Look at your marketing plan first. Make certain your profit centres and revenue streams are realistic. Focus on what you do that your customers like and need.

4. Determine if you need outside help. The business cemetery is filled with businesses that were too proud or too stupid to seek help.

5. Take emotion out of your business decisions. The successful turnaround does what is best for the company. Emotion-based decisions are often bad decisions. Successful turnarounds require long strings of good business decisions.

6. Assess the need to redesign the business. If your design is flawed, no amount of tweaking will bring quantum improvements.

7. Look carefully at staffing and personnel. If you have excess or non-productive employees, dismiss them as soon as possible. This should be done humanely and legally. Most importantly it should be done quickly. Non-productive employees can suck the blood out of a business. Successful turnarounds stop the bleeding quickly.

8. Determine your staffing/personnel needs. If you need new people, begin the hiring process immediately – even as you let non-producers go.

9. Make cash flow an integral part of the turnaround. If you do not have the numbers you need to monitor cash flow, find a way to get them. Ignorance of this area has killed many businesses.

10. Look carefully at payables. Know who needs what and when. Spreadsheets and software are the best ways to keep track of aged payables.

11. Look at each expense. Eliminate unnecessary expenses. Be careful if you cut expenses that bring value to your customers or clients. Make certain your payroll is covered. If you cannot meet payroll, you will not have the personnel to implement the turnaround. Do not forget taxes!

12. Look at receivables. Devise a plan to get paid. If your receivables plan is not working, find a way to improve or change it.

13. Change your turnaround plan as opportunities and problems change. Flexibility and swiftness are two key attributes in the successful turnaround.

14. Persevere. If you give up, so will your business.

Turnarounds are one of the most difficult things to accomplish in business. The pain and difficulty of a turnaround can only be offset by the incredible positive results a turnaround can bring. If your business is worth saving, you have to save it. If you cannot do what is required in a turnaround, then the writing is on the wall. Sell what you can before you lose it all, and start looking for a job. Maybe a company doing a turnaround can hire you.

Productivity

Of the many factors that contribute to the success of a business, few are as important as productivity. But what, precisely, is productivity in business? Productivity is the measure of output in relation to input – what a business produces that is of value to the customer compared to the resources invested. Yet productivity is a relative measurement. To illustrate this point, consider two companies, each producing virtually the same product. Company A produces more in absolute terms than company B, thus at first look company A would appear to be more productive than its competitor. Yet company B uses far less resources (input) than company A, so company B is actually the more productive of the two. Further, as company B continues to increase output without adding resources, it will become even more productive.

Rising productivity has been one of the most significant contributors to the strength of the US economy in recent years. This has enabled the USA to virtually eliminate inflation, despite increases in the wage base as well as certain goods and services.

Gains in productivity have largely offset these cost increases, keeping inflation in check and retaining the enormous confidence in the US economy which has prompted one of the most unstable stock markets that has ever been seen.

Savvy investors know that the future of the stock markets is substantially dependent on our ability to continue to achieve productivity gains. Continued improvements, however, will become increasingly difficult to achieve once most of the low-hanging fruit – the easy-to-get productivity gains – has been harvested. The USA's move from a post-Second World War industrial base to the 1990s world-based economy has taken place – now, however, the real work begins. Further increases in productivity will require companies to stretch higher by utilizing advanced techniques for improving productivity. To achieve this, we must demystify productivity. We must break this complicated, intimidating and potentially daunting concept into smaller components with easier-to-understand and manage tasks. Business owners and managers will require information about techniques for analysing and improving productivity in an organisation after the low-hanging fruit has been harvested. In the future, organizations are going to spend even more time following up on their performance. For productivity gains, the organization should try to set goals and follow the performance within the following areas:

- *Profitability*. How will profit, revenue, costs develop?
- *Business processes*. In this area, goals are set to support the completion of mapping activities of each process or to support developments for the improvement of their operations and efficiency.

- *Strategic planning.* Here it is important to measure the distribution and search for information both internally and externally.

- *Customer satisfaction.* Targets for improvement in different areas which will support the business objectives and develop customer relations include, for example, corporate image, corporate profile and customer satisfaction.

- *Leadership and human resource development.* Examples of indicators are: Staff have confidence in management. My manager is here when wanted. My manager is competent. My manager manages our unit. My manager develops his staff. My manager listens to and supports his staff

- *Information processing.* Data-processing and support consume a lot of resources and should be controlled.

- *Quality.* Quality is a business tool that may be used to quantify quality problems, reduce the cost of defective output and improve business processes. Armed with this information, companies can continue economic growth and stability – and companies can reap the rewards of productivity in an increasingly competitive world marketplace.

If productivity is defined as a measure of output in relation to input, it is a relatively simple matter to measure output. Output is the collective sum of products or services produced or provided by a business that its customers are willing to pay for. Input, however, is often much harder to identify and then control. Often, the most significant input in the production of a product or offering of a service is time. In most businesses, there are three types of time, each with a different impact on productivity. To truly understand and enhance productivity, the effect of all three types of time must be studied and managed.

Time

The first, and most commonly thought of, type of time is manpower time. Virtually every business employs people – whether direct or indirect production workers, office workers or executives – and the time spent by those people can be a significant input. Thus, whenever productivity improvement is mentioned, the natural inclination is to focus solely on manpower time. Much of the low-hanging fruit in this type of input has already been harvested through the use of automation, technology and lay-offs. Most managers feel that everything possible has been gained from this area. Indeed, industry journals are filled with mentions of increased stress, lean organizations and even deeper cutbacks. Careful analysis, however, will reveal that further increases in productivity are possible – without placing a further burden on the present workforce. The answer lies in working smarter instead of harder.

The second type of time is asset time. Most managers take assets – equipment, land, buildings, vehicles and use of capital – for granted. They fail to view assets as a true cost – on a par with labour, for example – yet nothing could be further from the truth. Just because equipment, buildings and the like do not draw a salary doesn't mean they come without cost. Their role, however, is often downplayed because the monthly income statement impact of assets is less apparent than that of manpower. Yet equipment that is not productively used, or warehouses that are filled with obsolete inventory, put just as much strain on the input side of the productivity equation as manpower does. Southwest Airlines uses this concept as one of its competitive advantages. By keeping its planes in the air most of the day, instead of sitting at gates and waiting, Southwest spreads its fixed asset costs over more flights and fare-paying passengers per day.

The third type of time – and the most recent entrant into the stream of management consciousness – is cycle time. Cycle time is defined as the elapsed time that starts when the first step of building a product is initiated, and ends when the product is ready for shipment to the customer. Since Toyota introduced the just-in-time (JIT) parts delivery concept to car manufacturing, the importance of cycle time has increased significantly. It has become one in a series of management buzz-words. Yet for all the strides made in recognizing this concept, the full appreciation of its impact on productivity still escapes most company managers. Why, they ask, would productivity be hurt by a longer cycle time, when the longer cycle time involves no additional manpower and no additional machine time? This kind of thinking can have a dramatic and negative, impact on productivity. Each type of input – manpower time, asset time and cycle time – has a separate, yet equal, importance.

Each type of input is divided into two parts: productive – the input which generates output – and non-productive – the input which generates no output. Productive input represents value – where time, energy and resources invested bear a return for that investment in the form of compensation by the customer. The customer buys the output and compensates the company for the effort involved in producing it. Non-productive input represents waste – time, energy and resources that are invested, but which generate no customer-demanded output. Yet even the segmentation of each type of time is not enough to generate meaningful improvements in productivity. To ensure greater understanding, non-productive time must be further divided into three distinct categories.

Waiting time is when manpower, assets or products are available for work/use but no value-added work is currently taking place. Non-value added time is when manpower, assets or products are working or being worked on, but such work does not add to the value of the finished product. Downtime is when workers or assets are not available for work due to illness, absences, breaks or machine malfunction, maintenance or changeovers. It is this categorization that helps organizations examine the various time elements that go into the production of a product or the offering of a service. And from this analysis, areas for improvement can be seen.

There are two different approaches to improving productivity – reducing or eliminating non-productive input, and enhancing the efficiency of productive input. Alone neither will provide the organization with the productivity increases necessary to sustain growth into the next century. Yet when taken together, these approaches will help the organization achieve its true potential. Non-productive time will be reduced, the 'black hole' will shrink dramatically, and the company's productivity will increase significantly.

The question remains: will industry take the next step in productivity improvement? Will it move past the low-hanging fruit and move higher, where picking is more difficult, but the rewards much sweeter? If this robust economy is to continue to thrive, it will have to.

Profit

Operating profit is profit before interest and tax but after deducting a management salary for the owner(s) which reflects a fair reward for their management activity (including overtime at home). The calculations below assume a safe investment return of 8 per cent and a borrowing cost of 12.5 per cent. Given these parameters, the operating profit should be at least 25 per cent of the operational investment in the company. Operational investment is fixed assets (ideally valued at replacement value) plus net current assets, which is stock, plus debtors (excluding any finance or tax balances), less creditors (excluding any finance or tax balances).

Getting started

The first decision you must make is, what business should I be in? More than anything else, the answer to this question will determine how successful you will be. This question can be broken down into three parts:

1. Should I be in business?

2. What business would I be most comfortable in?

3. What business could I make a profit in?

Let's deal with each part separately. To first determine whether you should be in business, it is helpful to look at the characteristics of a business executive. First and foremost, he is a risk-taker. No business venture is a sure thing, and the business executive recognizes this. That does not mean he plunges blindly into business. Rather, he assesses his chances, determines how much personal risk to take, and does as much preparatory work as possible to minimize the chance of failure.

A business executive is committed to her business. She is willing to spend as much time on it as is necessary. This may mean getting only four or five hours sleep a night. It may mean paying less attention to family and friends. It may mean working when she'd rather be doing something else. But the business executive knows the rewards of success, and this keeps her going. The business executive is determined, optimistic and resourceful. With eyes firmly fixed on success, she keeps working and smiling even when fate has delivered a kick to the business. And no matter how bad things look, she is willing and able to reason her way back to a successful course. She always has an idea to turn things around, or knows where to go to get help.

If you can truthfully say that you meet these criteria, then you have a future as a business executive. Once you know whether you have what it takes, you need to consider the type of business to be in. The first question to ask is what would I be most comfortable in and enjoy doing? It is important that you define a range of business activities you would enjoy undertaking. As a business executive, you will be spending many hours on your fledgling business, so you might as well enjoy it. However, since your favourite activity may not be profitable enough for you, you should have other alternatives which give you almost as much pleasure. Why the emphasis on enjoyment? Apart from the considerations mentioned above, it is easier for you to go the extra mile for a business you enjoy. It is much harder to be emotionally committed to the success of a company when you're in it only for the money. Business executives who have eyes only for dollars soon find that there aren't enough of them to compensate for hours spent and sacrifices made in the cause of their business. These business executives soon fail.

How should you determine what you enjoy? Think of all your skills and interests. Many of your skills would be appropriate to any business: communicating, decisiveness, clear thinking, cooperativeness and so on. However, some could provide business opportunities, too: the ability to work with your hands, good colour sense, mechanical aptitude, analytical thinking, the ability to carry out research, etc. Don't overlook specific technical skills, either. If you are a trained car mechanic, accountant, programmer, data entry person, lawyer or whatever, include that fact on your personal inventory.

What interests do you have? Gardening, playing cards, sailing, skiing, camping, sport, reading, listening to music, working with figures, driving, decorating, seeing films or woodworking, to name a few, are all interests that could provide a business opportunity. Once you become aware of them as interests, you have taken the first step towards basing a business on one of them.

Now, consider where your skills and interests overlap. Those areas form your range of business opportunities. Don't be surprised to find that you still have quite a long list; after all, part of the business executive's stock in trade is her wide interests and talents. At last, you are ready to decide what business would be most profitable for you. This is a two-part task. First, you must decide what is profitable enough, and then you must rate the various opportunities you have come up with. Your definition of profitability will rest on several criteria. First, how long are you willing to subsidize your business, and how much money are you willing to invest? Next, are you looking at a full-time involvement, or a part-time one? If you want to start out part-time with the intention of eventually working full-time, what is your deadline? Lastly, how much money do you need to take our of the business to live, and how much would you like to be able to take out?

The answers to those questions will tell you what profit level you want or need from your business, and will help you in your final determination of the business that is right for you.

In order to do this, you will need to analyse the opportunities you've come up with. The best way to do this is to determine what the market is for that kind of business, see whether it is growing, shrinking or holding its own, and find out about your potential competition: how many there are, how large they are, who they appear to be marketing to, and how successful they are. Once you have done all this, you will not only know what kind of business is most appropriate for you, you will also be well on your way to planning the success of that company.

Decision making

Having come this far in this book, you are now face to face with the single most essential activity of any business person: decision making.

The model we are presenting here has ten steps. They are:

1. Determining what decision you need to make.

2. Developing the decision criteria by which you will recognize the best decision.

3. Deciding how much of your resources (time, money, effort) you will commit.

4. Developing the relevant information.

5. Analysing that information.

6. Preparing a list of options.

7. Choosing the best option.

8. Planning your implementation process.

9. Putting your choice into effect.

10. Evaluating the success of your choice.

Case study 4.1 ABC Bakery Supply

Profitability

ABC Bakery Supply (ABC) is a $25 million distributor with frustrated management. The company distributes bakery supplies to customer segments that produce baked goods in a channel that is over 100 years old. Although their sales volume is about three times greater than the average for a distribution centre in the channel, the firm's gross margin (GM) of 18.05 per cent, operating profit margin of 1.15 per cent and number of stocking units (3,000+) are quite typical.

Here is what's bothering ABC's management:

1. The profit before interest and tax (PBIT) of $288,036 when divided by total assets in the business yields just over 5 per cent. If the shareholders liquidated the business and put their money into municipal bonds, they would get a better after-tax return on their investment and have 100 per cent leisure time, less financial risk and more borrowing liquidity. Why are they working so hard to make so little money with bigger risks?

2. The company is growing so slowly that it has been having trouble attracting and keeping good, new people. The 12 outside salespeople, for example, have an average age of 45, but figuring out how to renew sales energy is a growing concern.

3. Year-end supplier rebates for 2001 were roughly the entire PBIT total, and the trends aren't good. Over the last few years, the growth rates for sales, profits and rebates have all been declining.

Assumptions for growing profits

When asked, 'What are the company's assumptions for how to grow profits?' the following themes emerged from a management discussion:

1. Driving sales volume is vital. More volume earns more supplier rebates, better buying economics and more attention from producer reps that call on them. Fixed costs, which run at almost 20 per cent of all expenses, can be spread over more volume to allow more profit to get to the bottom line for an 'economy of scale'.

2. To get more sales, ABC has continued to hire more salespeople over the years to push into new territories and accounts. The salespeople generally push products and product promotion deals that are rolled out on a monthly basis, depending upon which suppliers were offering the best deals.

3. Maximizing the gross margin while keeping all operational costs to a bare minimum is vital. Salespeople are paid on a sliding scale percentage that goes up with the GM average for a territory.

After writing down these success assumptions, the following challenging questions were raised:

1. Where are the economies of scale from having three times the normal sales volume per distribution centre for the industry? Are the rest of the distributors doing worse? How much of the 'fixed costs' are really fixed? Do more of the overhead costs vary completely or partially with the number of employees needed for transactional activity or inventory and receivables to support more sales? (It turned out, for example, that half of the overhead costs had been interest on bank debt for inventory and receivables.)

2. How do GM% and GM$ per transaction relate to each other? What happens to the profits if the margin percentage drops a couple of points, but the order size goes up by over 50 per cent? When comparing average margin dollar per transaction with average cost per transaction, is it valid to just look at the 'incremental costs' of one more order? If, for example, the bottom 40 per cent of all transactions ranked by GM$ generated only 5 per cent of the GM$, but required 40 per cent of all activity costs (which is ABC's case!), then wouldn't any remaining fixed costs have to be allocated to each transaction? What should the firm do, if anything, to minimize the small order opportunity?

3. What does a ranking report of all customers by estimated PBIT contribution look like? Is it possible that profitability is driven more by an account's order-size economics first, then volume and margin per cent third? Is it possible that the specific product mix that a customer buys is a minor profitability issue? We know intuitively that an account that gets a small order delivery every day would be a definite loser. Are there any such accounts in the company's portfolio of customers?

4. Could the company have hit a level of diminishing returns? If salespeople and delivery lorries are driving further to smaller, more rural accounts that buy in smaller quantities, wouldn't the costs per sales call (estimated $100/call on average) and per stop rise while margin dollars per stop drop, to create more losing orders and customers?

5. Are there too many sales people calling on too many accounts that might be more effectively and efficiently covered by telemarketers or direct mail?

Analysis

To answer the above questions, the firm did the following analysis, and found some shocking things:

1. They ranked customers by PBIT using a 'quick-and-dirty, sufficiently accurate' method to find out that:

    (a) Four accounts generated 77 per cent of the total PBIT.

    (b) Five profitable territories out of 12 generated 206 per cent of the PBIT from 37 per cent of the accounts.

    (c) Seven unprofitable territories lost 106 per cent of the PBIT from the other 63 per cent of the accounts.

2. When looking at GM% for a territory, there was a slight bias towards lower GM% territories making more money, because their GM$ per transaction average was so much higher. The two highest GM% territories were both losers due to much lower average GM$ per transaction, but the current compensation scheme paid these salespeople the most.

3. For segmenting customers by sales volume per month or per year to qualify for different types of selling – (A) outside sales, (B) telemarketing, (C) direct mail, (D) cash-and-carry retail – management made the following assumptions:

    (a) For an outside salesperson to sell, instal and maintain a 'lowest total procurement cost (TPC) replenishment system' for a customer, he would have to call on an account at least once a month. The account would therefore have to produce a minimum of $24,000 in sales per year in order to keep the ratio of sales expense to GM$ at 25 per cent or less. Only 256 accounts out of 1,105 active accounts exceeded this figure.

(b) Using the same logic pattern for telemarketing coverage, an account would have to make between $12,000 and $24,000 in sales per year. Only 187 accounts fell within this annual sales range.

(c) For the next two strata of accounts, the 'C'/direct mail and 'D'/retail accounts the numbers were 501 and 200 respectively.

Psychological resistance

Management was generally disbelieving of what the different reports suggested. How tough is it to admit that you have been working so hard with the wrong assumptions for the last 20 years? They attacked the activity-based costing model for computing PBIT per customer. A second round of analysis revealed that 'fixed overhead' costs were mostly variable or semi-variable. After making and testing every assumption that could be raised to make the extremely profitable and unprofitable accounts less so, the net result was that both groups were still extreme. The PBIT ranking was sufficiently accurate, it turns out, to start rethinking the entire customer portfolio around PBIT/customer and segmenting them for different types of selling.

The next wave of resistance involved questions relating to: 'How are we going to rethink all of our sales/marketing methods?' What would the sales force say? A new compensation system would have to be designed, and fewer outside salespeople would be needed to call on at most 300 customers who qualified as 'A' or potential 'A' accounts. None of the salespeople could explain the '11 elements of total procurement cost' let alone sell, instal and maintain a system that would both lower buying and selling costs for a sustainable win–win relationship. They were all addicted to 'selling' special-price or incentive product promotions. And the firm had no real telemarketing expertise for the 'B' account coverage.

Wouldn't suppliers be upset too? The company would have to stop doing most of the promotions that conflicted in principle with the TPC purchasing system theory. What if sales growth dropped over the next year by 2–5 per cent because some customers switched to the competition instead of changing their buying behaviour to become profitable to ABC? Wouldn't manufacturing representative income take hits? Yes, but what if profits quadrupled and target customer penetration growth started to accelerate at a superior rate after six to nine months? Were there other positive possibilities?

Brainstorming about what could work for most profitable, most unprofitable and best target accounts raised spirits. Management agreed that if they visited the most profitable customers, the odds were good that the company could find new ways to better serve, protect and penetrate those accounts. Then the same new insights could be applied to the next most promising target accounts. If all the employees knew these franchise and target accounts by heart and had permission to give them extra service as needed, it could make a big difference in growing and keeping them.

As for the biggest losing accounts, they were simply placing lots of small orders that were killing both parties with a number of costs. Most of these accounts just needed help in adjusting their reorder points, reorder quantities and paperwork processing to save costs on both sides. For some of these accounts, the hope was to use the audit adjusting process as a way to gain more volume. The odds seemed good that most of the dramatic losers could be turned into solid winners, which would lead to a big swing in company profitability.

What next?

All of the resistance was eventually boiled down to a simple choice. 'Should we keep on doing what we are doing: working hard, making no money and watching the boat sink? Or should we forge ahead with new profitability assumptions and methods for which we just have to be one level better than the competitors to unleash new profit growth?'

What do you think they should do? Do you have similar opportunities buried under a lot of empty, even unprofitable, activity within your business? How should you better educate yourself and your employees about rethinking your profitability assumptions and using new methods to quadruple profits and accelerate growth rates?

CHAPTER 5

Supporting changes in the business

At every stage of the change process, people must feel that senior management are fully and visibly behind their efforts. There are a number of things you can do to demonstrate your support.

- *Clarify goals.* Carefully define the goals – the necessary outcomes of the change effort. Develop criteria for a quality change process, but hold realistic expectations about the nature of potential outcomes, the time and resources required, and the risk. Make managers accountable both for demonstrable change results and for meeting normal business goals during the design and implementation periods.

- *Develop a strategy.* Develop a realistic strategy for change, one that involves all affected functions. Assess the overall readiness of the organization, for example the levels of understanding, trust and stress. Work to remove major blocks before beginning. Allocate the proper resources – time, people, consultants, budget.

- *Appreciate the complexity.* Recognize that this effort means changes in the work system (mission, goals, technology, structure, roles, skills, rewards); culture (values, beliefs, norms, practices); and politics (basis for power, coalitions, resources, who wins/loses, perception of fairness).

- *Set up the planning and managing structure.* Establish the appropriate planning and managing structure (steering committees, design teams, task groups). Insist upon high performance standards for every group that is part of the change process.

- *Get top-level support.* Convince upper management that this change effort is the right thing to do. Be sure that corporate policies, systems and contracts (employment security, compensation, personnel policies, union contracts) support the change process. Get assurances that top-level people will support the change effort and will not try to block it.

- *Use good people.* Assign competent people to the change effort. Keep key managers in place, at least through the early stages of implementation. Choose successors, when required, for skill in continuing the effort.

- *Involve all management.* Ensure that the middle and lower management groups are heavily involved in influencing the change process. Frequently their jobs are affected. They need to learn about their options and the skills they will need.

- *Guide the change process.* Monitor, guide, support and protect the change effort. Coach, critique and reward those directly involved. Ask tough questions; provide feedback; maintain high standards. Keep the design process focused on the vision. Be a teacher, an intellectual leader. Make mid-course corrections when needed during implementation, but be sure to distinguish between defects in the design and shortcomings in the implementation plan.

- *Keep things moving.* Keep the effort moving ahead even when unexpected setbacks occur. Don't abandon ship when the seas get rough; beef up the resources if necessary. Remind people of the vision to ensure it remains a powerful incentive to change. Address difficult issues as they arise so that frustration does not build. But don't move so rapidly that large numbers of people are left behind.

- *Demonstrate commitment.* Personally demonstrate ownership of and commitment to the change effort. Articulate and practise the beliefs that underpin the new organization. Model a personal style that enables, energizes and facilitates. Act in a way that is consistent with the vision. Talk to people; listen to their concerns and suggestions. Give the change effort prominence on every agenda.

- *Help people learn.* When things go wrong (and they will), help the people who own the problem to understand and deal with the issues that caused the problem. Do not revert to the expert role and introduce quick solutions – this will provide little learning for the organization and will foster dependency. Sometimes it is better to ask questions than to give answers. Also, be sure that people understand that, while mistakes will occur, they are not going to derail the change process.

- *Make change visible.* Work to make change visible as soon as possible. Visible changes might include a shift in the overall management style, the distribution of more business information, involvement of more people in problem solving, visits to customers and improvement of facilities. Demonstrate your good intentions early on.

- *Empower people.* Begin to empower people at all levels. To unlock their energy: share information; encourage the development of knowledge, skills and competence; push responsibility and authority down; encourage initiative and innovation; respond positively to it; provide the necessary resources (tools, technology, time, information, training, budget); acknowledge achievement; provide rewards; develop a sense of common purpose, community, teamwork; value, build and take advantage of a diverse workforce; and provide appropriate directions, goals, coaching, support, feed-back and mentoring.

- *Celebrate gains.* Focus on and celebrate positive accomplishments: recognize successes.

Developing a leadership team

Leading the organization design effort requires a major shift in leadership roles, personal style and teamwork. Senior leaders can rightfully be expected to model the key behaviours that will eventually be required of all organization members, for example learning, teamwork, participating, delegation and collaboration across boundaries.

- *Change roles.* Work out the senior management role for the change process – what to be personally involved in and what to delegate. Also, begin thinking about and preparing for the permanent role changes that will occur when the new design is implemented, such as delegation of decision making, coaching and more time spent planning.

- *Change style.* Recognize that the new organization will require changes in the values, behaviour and instincts of senior management. Define the new competencies they will need, for example interpersonal competence, team leadership and conflict management. Begin building and using these leadership skills at the very start of the change effort. Few managers are born with a natural participative style; they need time and experience to build competence so that they can provide leadership to the new organization.

- *Develop the team.* Become a more effective senior management team. Functional heads at the top must learn to work well together if their subordinates are to mesh into smooth working teams on the shop floor, in the lab or in the office. Seek frequent feedback on the effectiveness of the leadership team.

- *Require learning.* Stress to managers the need for continuous, aggressive learning. Change requires courageous leaders who can deal with complexity and uncertainty.

Typical reactions to change

- *Disengagement.* Some people in the system may resist by disengaging or withdrawing from the process. They may distance themselves and show little interest or initiative in implementing or cooperating with the change. Though they may quit altogether, typically they stay, giving no energy to the new process. Their response might be to minimize what is happening: this is just another fad. It will blow over. Don't avoid those who draw back. Instead, be direct in engaging them about the change, and listen to and explore their concerns with them.

- *Disidentification.* Other people may have important aspects of their own identity tied to the previous ways of doing things and the roles they played that now seem threatened. They may say, 'I wasn't consulted so don't blame me'. Or, 'I used to ...' Because they identify with a particular way of doing things, it is helpful to explore how they can get what they need and want, and feel valued in a new system with new ways.

- *Disorientation.* When new approaches are introduced, disorientation is a common response. Some will be confused about new procedures and about how they will fit in. They may not grasp how these changes reflect a shift in the priorities and direction of the company. They may say, 'I don't get this. What are we supposed to do?' Information, explanations and direction help the disoriented.

- *Disenchantment.* Those who respond with disenchantment perhaps recognize most clearly that real change is occurring – that some ways are disappearing to make way for something new. Their reaction can be one of anger, negativity and sometimes even sabotage: 'This won't work'. 'It's awful!' Their anger needs to be heard, acknowledged and dealt with so that they can move through it.

Strategies for changing systems

- Involve others in the process and seek a shared vision.
- Take time to build shared ownership.
- Avoid quick fixes.
- Be respectful of the different ways people respond to change.
- Remember that change takes time.
- Don't be afraid to take risks or to innovate.
- Be accountable and direct. Build trust throughout the system.
- Be realistic in your demands on the time of others.
- Clarify roles and lines of accountability and follow them.
- Don't build unhealthy dependencies into the system.

- Thank and support others.

- Build on the strengths of current systems rather than berating them. They met the needs of their time. Times are changing.

- Demonstrate and communicate measurable results.

- Don't become so concerned with the mechanics of change that you lose concern for people.

- Accept the idea that the first person who needs to change is you.

Decision making

There is a great deal of literature on decision making, and there are a number of models available, but the steps presented above are, we have found, very useful and easily understood. Let's look at each of the steps in turn.

When you decide what decision you must make, it is important that you examine the problem, question or opportunity in great detail. Make sure that you are addressing the central issue, not something which, while it may seem obvious, is really only a symptom or side issue.

Once you know the decision to be made, you need to be able to recognize the best course of action. You need to have decision criteria. So ask yourself: if I were to make this decision, what results would I see? Those become your decision criteria. To be successful, the alternative would have to produce the results you have identified. Now comes a tough part: allocating your resources. How much of your available time, effort and money are you willing and able to commit to making this particular decision? You may have heard the term paralysis by analysis. It probably refers to people or organizations who have large amounts of resources to devote to making decisions and who, as a result, spend far too much time and energy on matters which are relatively irrelevant. You, on the other hand, will look at the importance of the decision, the amount of time available and the size of your resource pool, and decide, based on that, how much of your resources you will commit. This is your budget, and you should stick to it.

The next step is searching out the relevant information. The test for relevance is: does this information deal directly with the decision I need to make, or is it only tangential or even unrelated? Time spent with irrelevant data is time wasted, so be sure you are dealing with only important information. It is also wise to set a limit to the time you spend on getting information. Data-gathering can go on forever, since you never have all the information you need. So determine what is relevant, then what is most important, then where it can be found, collect it and summarize it.

Analysis is the next step. Look at the information you have gathered in the light of the decision you need to make. Does it have a positive or negative effect on your decision? As you analyse, some other solutions will begin to suggest themselves. Make a note of them and, when you are ready, test them and any others you have thought of, to see if they address the central issue on which you must decide. If they do, they are viable options. Flush each one out to see how it would work. This will give enough information on each to enable you to make your choice.

Selecting the best alternative should be easy. It is the one which best deals with the central issue, most closely satisfies your decision criteria, and which can be implemented with the least net cost and greatest potential profit (where profit is a consideration).

Implementation design involves splitting the decision into major tasks to be accomplished, dividing each task into easily achieved subtasks, deciding what resources you will assign to each task (time, people, money, etc.). Develop a schedule for implementation and decide how you will know whether you have successfully achieved your goals (building in milestones or measurements of interim progress). Then, you have nothing else to do but get on with implementing your plan. Roll up your sleeves and begin work.

Finally, evaluation means sitting down and seeing whether your decision was successfully implemented. Did it do what it was supposed to? Why, or why not? Did it create other opportunities for decision making? What are they? And, with that question, you are ready to start the whole process over again.

Products and services

In this section, you must give a full description of the products or services you intend to market so you have a clear idea of your intentions. You may want to emphasize any unique features of your product. Be specific in showing how you will give your business a competitive edge.

1. How does your product or service differ from the competition?

2. What are the main features of your product or service?

3. At what point is your product entering the life-cycle?

4. What message will you include on your package?

5. What will be the size, shape, colour and material of the package?

6. What are your sales and production forecasts?

Discuss future products or services that you may offer, including research and development plans as well as future expansion plans.

Metrics

Metrics is a synonym for measurement. It's been said, if you don't know where you are going, any road will get you there. It is the same with measurement. You need to know whether your organization is healthy or unhealthy. You want to eliminate the mistakes of the past. You need to evaluate your organization's past, present and future. This section defines and provides guidance on the use of metrics to aid continuous performance improvement for your organization.

Understanding metrics

A basic definition of metrics is the specific measurement of an entity that can be used to predict, evaluate, guide, forewarn, inform and provide a basis for action. Metrics can be both qualitative and quantitative in nature. In addition, metrics can be placed into three main categories: (1) process (project) (e.g. schedule); (2) product (e.g. reliability); and (3) hybrid (e.g. change orders). However, these categories should not be taken as all-inclusive. Good metrics must be realistic and worthwhile to the user; are typically linked to a goal or a strategy; cause action, not reaction; focus attention on the few critical issues that will determine success from failure; should be used in real time to inform and to instruct; and allow the user to detect and correct potential problems before they become real problems.

Really good metrics must be able to take the temperature of your organization. To do this, you must rethink the way you measure your organization's performance:

- Fewer is better: concentrate on measuring the vital few key variables rather than the trivial many.

- Measures should be linked to the factors needed for success.

- Measures should be a mix of past, present and future to ensure that the organization is concerned with all three perspectives.

- Measures should be based around the needs of customers, shareholders and other key stakeholders.

- Measures should start at the top and flow down to all levels of employees in the organization.

- Multiple indices can be combined into a single index to give a better overall assessment of performance.

- Measures should be changed or at least adjusted as the environment, and your strategy, change.

- Measures need to have targets or goals established that are based on research rather than arbitrary numbers.

Strategic measurement model: key factors

Mission, vision and values

Remember, measurement is easy. What is difficult is measuring the right things and ignoring irrelevant data. The organization must define what it is and what it stands for.

Key success factors and business fundamentals.

This is the stage where the organization focuses on the key factors that differentiate it from its competition. Business fundamentals are those things like profitability, growth or regulation. They are the major strengths or weaknesses that should be exploited or corrected.

Performance metrics

A natural outflow of the success factors will be measurements selected by the company to index critical areas for success. There should only be a few.

Goals/objectives

Goals or objectives should be set for each metric. These goals should be based on research and need to link up well together. Linking the goals will ensure that one measure does not cause a negative reaction with another measure.

Strategies

Once the goals and objectives have been identified, then the organization can identify strategies and action plans that will allow these goals to be achieved.

No guarantee of success

Redesigning a company's measurement system will not guarantee success. This is not just another fad. It doesn't matter if you are a large or small organization; your scorecards will be bad if you choose the wrong metrics.

Benefits of implementing strategic measurement

Below are the benefits of a good set of metrics that will improve your organization's scorecard:

- 80 per cent reduction in monthly volume of reports;
- 50 per cent reduction in the amount of time spent in senior management meetings;
- 60 per cent reduction in the number of reports printed daily;
- increase in the ability to focus on long- and short-term goals;

- better balance between the needs of the customer, shareholders and employees;
- elimination of hours of time spent by managers reviewing unimportant performance data;
- ability to track vision and values of employees.

Seven ways to make sure your measurement system fails

1. *Make sure you collect too much data.* Get hundreds and hundreds of minute details. Make sure your employees have so much data that they have no time to do real work.

2. *Make sure you focus on the wrong data.* Make sure that the only types of data you evaluate are financial and operational. This is short-term stuff. Focus on this and you will fail. What you really need to look at is employee and customer satisfaction, product and service quality and public safety measures.

3. *Lack of detail.* This can be just as bad a trap as too much detail.

4. *Pick measures that drive the wrong performance.* How do you measure intellectual work products? It's very difficult to find measurements for information, ideas, removing problems and finding solutions. How many pages per day a person writes to meet a superficial performance standard is not important. What is important is how many *good* pages are written a day.

5. *Place more importance on courtesy than on competency.* Just saying hello or smiling isn't going to mean anything if your people aren't competent. A better measure is sales and repeat customers – that's what counts.

6. *Put greater importance on how a person looks than what they produce.* Who cares about a person's appearance? The real concern is how well they perform. The problem with measuring behaviours is what you ask for isn't going to ensure the quality of the finished product.

7. *Pick measures that discourage teamwork and encourage competition.* How often do business units within companies compete against one another? Even performance evaluations that rate a person against their contemporaries encourage competition between members of the same organization, and thus redirect energy away from the organization's real goals.

CHAPTER 6

Balanced scorecards

Here are seven recommendations for balanced scorecard measurements:

- customer satisfaction
- employee satisfaction
- financial performance
- operational performance
- product/service quality
- supplier performance
- safety/environmental/public responsibility.

Balanced scorecards

Balanced scorecards provide a framework around which an organization can change its strategy. This is accomplished by linking everything together.

- *Cascading.* This is the process of taking a pilot scorecard (usually at the operating business unit level) and moving the entire process into other parts of the organization.

- *Cause–effect relationship.* The natural flow of business performance from a lower level to an upper level within or between perspectives. For example, training employees in customer relations leads to better customer service, which in turn leads to improved financial results. One side is the driver, producing an outcome on the other side.

- *Goal.* An overall achievement that is considered critical to the future success of the organization. Goals express where the organization wants to be.

- *Measurement.* A way of monitoring and tracking the progress of strategic objectives. Measurements can be drivers of performance (leading to outcomes) or outcomes.

- *Objective.* What, specifically, must be done to execute the strategy, i.e. what is critical to the future success of our strategy? What must the organization do to reach its goals?

- *Perspectives.* Four or five strategic areas that define why and how the organization exists. Perspectives provide a framework for measurement. The four most common perspectives are financial (final outcomes), customer, internal processes, and learning and growth.

- *Programmes.* Major initiatives that must be undertaken in order to meet one or more strategic objectives.

- *Strategic map.* A logical framework for organizing a collection of strategic objectives over four or more perspectives. Everything is linked to capture a cause and effect relationship. Strategic maps are the foundation for building the balanced scorecard.

- *Strategy.* An expression of what the organization must do to get from one reference point to another reference point. Strategy is often expressed in terms of a mission statement, vision, goals or objectives. Strategy is usually developed at the top levels of the organization, but executed by lower levels within the organization.

- *Target.* An expected level of performance or improvement required in the future.

- *Templates.* Visual tools for assisting people with building a balanced scorecard, typically used for capturing and comparing data within the four components of the balanced scorecard: strategic maps, measurements, targets and programmes.

- *Vision.* An overall statement of how the organization wants to be perceived over the long term (three to five years).

Now that you understand the basic structure and terminology behind the balanced scorecard, let's describe the overall process of building it. The process consists of six steps in two phases.

Phase I: the strategic foundation

Step 1. Establish your strategic goals. Goals need to be specific so that they can be linked into the scorecard. Therefore, strategic goals or destination statements represent the anchor for the remainder of the entire process. Example: 'Over the next two years, we will expand our overall market share by 25 per cent.'

Step 2. Define your strategic themes. Most organizations operate around a set of strategic themes, such as customer service, product development and operational efficiency.

Step 3. Build a strategic map for each (see step 2). Out of all the steps in the entire process, this is the most difficult. You need to map out a set of strategic objectives over four perspectives for each strategic theme.

Phase II: critical components

Step 4. Establish measurements. For each strategic objective on each strategic map there needs to be at least one measurement. Measurement provides feedback on whether or not you are meeting your strategic objectives.

Step 5. Set targets for each measurement. For each measurement in your scorecard, set a target. Targets establish a desired outcome in the future.

Step 6. Launch programmes. Things will not happen unless the organization undertakes formal change programmes, initiatives or projects. This effectively closes the loop and links you back to where you started.

Don't worry if all of this doesn't make sense yet! Once you have read this chapter, you should have a solid understanding of what is required for building a balanced scorecard.

Strategic goals or destination statements should:

1. Go to the heart of why the organization exists.

2. Have solid agreement from all stakeholders.

3. Be specific enough to establish some way of measuring how well you are doing.

4. Paint a picture of where your organization will be at some point in time.

5. Validate and clarify the organization's vision.

Figure 6.1 illustrates a customer focused process for profitability.

Goals come from your vision, mission and other strategy statements. Most goals will be rooted in what the organization has done in the past and what it is hoping to do in the future. Best practices, benchmarking and other analytical research can be used to help define goals. You can also refer to the following sources when developing your goals:

- strategic plans

- marketing plans

- financial plans

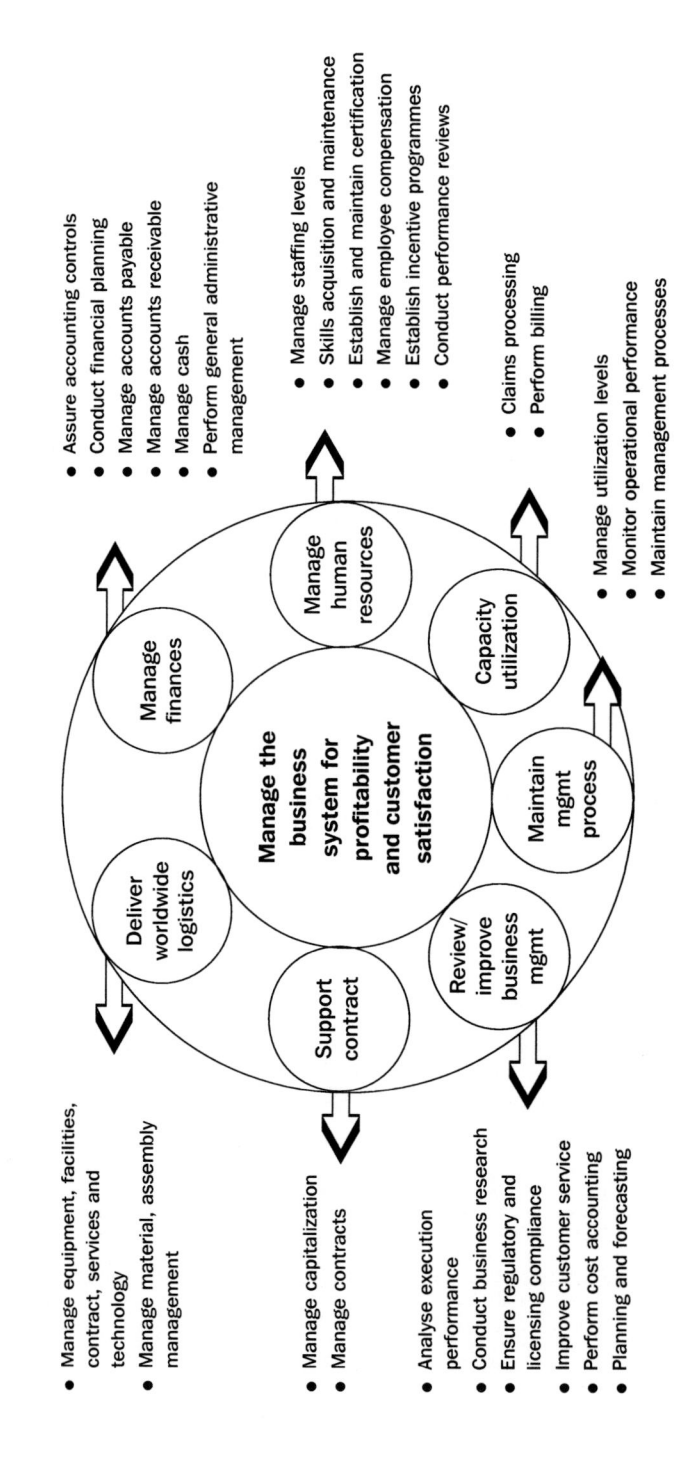

- Manage equipment, facilities, contract, services and technology
- Manage material, assembly management

- Manage capitalization
- Manage contracts

- Analyse execution performance
- Conduct business research
- Ensure regulatory and licensing compliance
- Improve customer service
- Perform cost accounting
- Planning and forecasting

- Assure accounting controls
- Conduct financial planning
- Manage accounts payable
- Manage accounts receivable
- Manage cash
- Perform general administrative management

- Manage staffing levels
- Skills acquisition and maintenance
- Establish and maintain certification
- Manage employee compensation
- Establish incentive programmes
- Conduct performance reviews

- Claims processing
- Perform billing

- Manage utilization levels
- Monitor operational performance
- Maintain management processes

Figure 6.1 A customer-focused profitability process.

- budgets
- human resource management plans and policies
- quality control programmes
- competitive analysis
- industry trend analysis.

Once you have established your strategic goals (see Table 6.1), a set of strategic themes should emerge. For example, suppose you have the following destination statement: 'We will grow revenues by 35 per cent over the next three years.' This goal relates to financial results. Financial results lead to improved shareholder value. Therefore, improving shareholder value through higher revenues is your strategic theme.

Strategic themes are well defined, separable, focused in relation to action required, achievable, support overall strategic direction and imply some degree of change or impact on the organization. Strategic themes tend to cut across the four perspectives that make up the balanced scorecard. Referring back to our example on

Table 6.1 Determining your strategic goals

Basis for determining your goal	Description of goal
Past performance – what do shareholders expect from us?	Over the next two years, we will grow our revenue base by 45 per cent
Industry trends – where is the overall industry moving?	We will position our company to be the leading provider of wireless Internet access within two years
Competitive analysis – what are the best practices in our industry?	By the year 2004, we will be ranked number one in customer service

growing revenues by 35 per cent, Table 6.2 shows how this maps down the scorecard.

Table 6.2 Basic flow of strategic theme within the balanced scorecard

Shareholder value	
Financial	Revenue growth
Customer	More customers
Processes	Customer marketing and service programmes
Learning	Support systems and personnel

As illustrated in Table 6.2, strategic themes tend to generate a string of strategic objectives for populating the balanced scorecard. At the same time, they link with the strategic goals (see Table 6.3).

Table 6.3 Example of linking a strategic goal to a strategic theme

Strategic goal = →	By 2005, our company will have the most innovative product line of hand-held computers
↑	↓
Strategic theme = →	Product innovation

The four most common strategic themes are:

- growing the business
- operational excellence
- customer relations
- product innovation.

Now that the strategic goals or destinations are established (Step 1) and now that we have identified our strategic themes (Step 2), we will construct a strategic map for each theme from Step 2. As you may recall, we noted that balanced scorecards are structured over four perspectives or layers: financial, customer, internal processes and learning and growth. Strategic maps will all include these four layers. Within each layer, we will place our strategic objectives, making sure everything links back. Trying to develop strategic objectives and placing them into the correct layers for all strategic maps is probably the most difficult step in building the balanced scorecard. Consultants sometimes refer to this step as straw modelling: trying to string together connecting lines over a map that presents an overall strategic model.

Strategic mapping starts at the very top – strategic goals and themes. For example, most publicly traded companies have shareholder value as a strategic theme. In order to improve shareholder value, the organization can do things like grow revenues or increase productivity. Once you decide on your strategy for improving shareholder value, then you have to decide on how you will grow revenues or increase productivity. Table 6.4 illustrates this top-down flow within the financial perspective.

We will flow our strategic objectives down each perspective within the map, making sure everything is linked. This is how we build the balanced scorecard strategic map.

Next, we move down to the customer perspective. In order to map the customer perspective, we need to understand the value(s) we provide to our customers. For example, Federal Express is extremely efficient at getting packages delivered on time. Therefore

Table 6.4 Mapping strategic objectives within the financial perspective

Shareholder value			
Grow revenues ↑		↑ Increase productivity	
↑	↑	↑	↑
New sources of revenues	Increase customer profitability	Lower costs	High utilization of assets

on-time delivery is the specific value that Federal Express delivers to its customers. Companies that emphasize operational efficiency usually provide one or more value attributes: price, quality, time or selection. Other companies may create value for customers through their great relationship with the customer. Finally, some companies may add value by emphasizing innovative and unique products and/or services. It is extremely important to define your customer and the values you provide; otherwise you run the risk of building a scorecard that doesn't fit with the capabilities of the organization.

Referring back to the customer perspective, we could choose between three strategies:

1. Operational efficiency – value for customers through price, quality, time or selection.

2. Customer relationships – value for customers through personal service, building trust, brand loyalty, providing customized solutions and other one-to-one relationships.

3. Innovative products and services – inventing new products and features, fast delivery of products and services, forming partnerships to expand product lines and other product leadership initiatives.

Customer perspective. The customer perspective enables organizations to align the core measure (customer satisfaction) to targeted customers. For this perspective, the primary objectives are to provide effective service to and establish effective partnerships with external and internal customers. Effective service and partnerships are key ingredients in assessing the health of any management programme.

Internal business processes perspective. The objectives in the internal business processes perspective collectively ensure that an effective management programme is established to (1) support customer needs; (2) provide efficient life-cycle management (accountability, utilization and disposition) of direct operations personal property; and (3) maintain oversight of entities that have programme responsibilities. Key processes in this programme must be monitored to ensure that the outcomes satisfy programme objectives.

Learning and growth. The two objectives under the learning and growth perspective promote organizational and individual growth that will provide long-term benefits to the personal property management programme. These objectives must be achieved if programme performance is going to improve over time. While the objectives in the other perspectives identify where the programme must excel to achieve breakthrough performance, the learning and growth objectives provide the infrastructure needed to enable the objectives in the other perspectives to be achieved. The learning and growth objectives are the drivers for achieving excellence in the other perspectives.

Financial perspective. The objective of the financial perspective is to strive for optimum efficiency in the personal property management programme. To achieve that, processes need to be analysed to determine (1) cost and performance trends over time and (2) process changes that can be implemented to produce optimum efficiencies. Success for entities charged with personal property management programme responsibilities should be measured by how effectively and efficiently these entities meet the needs of their constituencies.

This perspective is important because optimizing the cost efficiency of the personal property management programme ensures that the maximum amount of funds are available for accomplishing the primary missions of the department and its field organizations. Managers must ensure that operating costs are optimized in order to meet the challenge of creating business programmes that work better and cost less.

Phase I is summarized in Table 6.5.

Table 6.5 Summary of Phase I

Four major milestones – Phase I	
1st	Establish your strategic goals.
2nd	Identify three to five strategic themes.
3rd	Develop a set of critical strategic objectives.
4th	Build the balanced scorecard strategic map(s).

Measurements on your strategic map

For each strategic objective on your strategic map, you need at least one measurement. If you have several measurements for a strategic objective, then the chances are you have more than one strategic objective. Can you have an objective without a measurement? It is possible, but not having a measurement makes it difficult to manage the objective. It's best to revisit this objective and ask the question: 'Why is this an objective?'

Measurement provides feedback on how well you are doing in meeting your strategic objectives. Measurement conveys action, giving direction on what needs to be accomplished. Measurement is a continuous test of the strategy, asking the question: 'How valid is the strategy?'

So, how do you build your measurements? Here are some basic guidelines. Measurements should be:

- *Focused* – measurements communicate what is strategically important.

- *Repeatable* – measurements are repeatable over time, allowing comparisons.

- *Useful* – measurements are useful for establishing targets.

- *Accountable* – measurements are reliable, verifiable and accurate.

- *Frequent* – measurements are available when needed.

The measurement template shown in Table 6.6 can be used to help build an appropriate measurement.

Table 6.6 Measurement template

Strategic objective →	
Describe the measurement →	
Define type/formula →	
Unit of measurement →	
Frequency of measurement →	
Assumptions →	
Sources →	
Availability →	___ Available ___ Not available ___ Requires change
Support required →	___ IT support ___ Finance support ___ Other

In addition to the above criteria, you need to understand some concepts related to measurement. For example, some measurements will drive change in your organization. These types of measurements are often called leading indicators (drivers) since they drive or push final outcomes within the organization. Examples include customer contracts executed, competitive pricing index, employee feedback indicator, service response time and time spent with customers. If your organization needs to change rapidly, then you need to include some leading measurements in your balanced scorecard. A common place to use drivers (leading measurements) is within the learning and growth perspective since this is the principal driver perspective behind the balanced scorecard.

The other side of measurement is historical measurements that show us an outcome. These measurements are usually referred to as lagging indicators and they dominate most performance measurement systems. About 70 per cent of all measurements fall into this category. Examples include most financial measurements (return on equity, sales growth, economic value added, etc.) and many non-financial measurements (production breakeven, customer retention, employee productivity index, etc.). Outcome or lagging measurements are common within the customer and financial perspectives since these are outcome-related.

A good rule is to extrapolate about 50 per cent of your measurements from existing systems and procedures. Some common measurements include ratios, percentages, ratings, rankings and indices. Ratios are good for expressing critical relationships, while percentages are good for expressing an overall trend over time. Rankings work well for highly ranked companies trying to move up in the ranking. However, lower ranked companies usually cannot move easily within a ranking system and, therefore, this form of measurement may be too ambitious.

Another way to look at measurement is to understand the relationship between drivers and outcomes for the three lower perspectives. For example, the customer perspective can be broken down into two groups of measurement: core measurements (customer satisfaction, retention, market share, customers acquired and customer profitability) and performance drivers (competitive pricing, excellent quality, outstanding reputation, image and customer relationships). In order to retain customers, we must provide one or more value attributes to the customer (see Table 6.7).

The internal process perspective can be broken down into three outcome categories:

- *Outcome 1* – innovative processes that meet customer needs, provide solutions and address emerging trends. Example of driver measurement: number of new products introduced.

Table 6.7 Core vs. driver measurements for the customer perspective

Customer perspective	Outcome measurements from the drivers				
	Customer satisfaction Customer retention Market share				
	Drivers – Value attributes provided to customers:				
	Quality	Time	Price	Image	Reputation

- *Outcome 2* – operations that produce and deliver products and services to customers. Example of driver measurement: delivery response time to customer.

- *Outcome 3* – value-added services provided to customers once products and/or services have been delivered. Example of driver measurement: cycle time for resolving customer complaint.

The learning and growth perspective emphasizes three outcome categories: employees, systems and organization.

- *Outcome 1* – employee satisfaction, productivity and retention. Example of driver measurement: percentage of key personnel turnover.

- *Outcome 2* – systems – engaging to the end user, accessibility and quality of information. Example of driver measurement: percentage of employees who have online access.

- *Outcome 3* – organization – climate for change, strong leadership, empowering the workforce and other motivating factors.

Example of driver measurement: number of employee suggestions.

One of the major challenges in building your balanced scorecard is to keep the number of measurements to a manageable few. Throughout building the balanced scorecard, we try to follow the 'four to five rule'. This rule says that we should build balanced scorecards with four to five layers, four to five measurements per layer, resulting in no more than 20 to 25 measurements per scorecard. If you have too many measurements, you can index your measurements into one single measurement. For example, you can apply weighted percentages to calculate a single measurement (see Table 6.8).

Table 6.8 Weighted example

Measurement description	Value	Importance	Index
Customer satisfaction rating	0.78	50%	0.39
Customer compliment index	0.89	25%	0.22
Quality satisfaction indicator	0.72	25%	0.18
Single measurement used in balanced scorecard			0.79

However, indexing is a double-edged sword. It helps to reduce the number of measurements necessary, but it also buries the results, making it difficult to clearly see what is going on. The best approach is to use stand-alone measurements wherever possible.

One of the best benchmarks to apply to your measurements is to ask the following question: 'Can I understand your strategic objective by simply looking at your measurement?' Keep in mind that you are trying to capture the possible best cause and effect relationship. This is what makes a great balanced scorecard. For example, what does the measurement 'per cent sales growth' say? It implies that we have a strategic objective that must be related to growing sales revenues. Suppose your strategic objective was not to increase sales revenues, but to increase return on shareholder equity. This changes your measurement to return on equity. Remember that everything must be linked as you build your balanced scorecard.

Measurement alone is not enough. We must drive behavioural changes within the organization if we expect to change strategy. This requires establishing a target for each measurement within the balanced scorecard. Targets are designed to stretch and push the organization to meet its strategic objectives. Suppose the strategic objective is to improve customer satisfaction and the measurement is based on the number of customer complaints. Imagine that the average number of monthly complaints was 45 for the last 12 months. A target of no more than 40 complaints could be established. Targets need to be realistic so that people feel comfortable about trying to achieve them. Therefore targets should be mutually agreed between management and the person held responsible for hitting the target. One good place to start in setting a target is to look at past performance. Your strategic goals can also give you clues as to what your targets should be. Another good source for targets is benchmarking for best practices. See Table 6.9.

Make sure your targets match your measurements, communicating what needs to change in relation to the measurement. Also be aware that targets may require considerable research before they can

Table 6.9 Setting targets based on strategic goals

Current year sales revenues	Goal: We will grow sales by 40% over the next 3 years		
	2002 target	*2003 target*	*2004 target*
$160,000	$172,000	$195,000	$224,000

be set. Finally, if past targets have not resulted in much change, then you should consider setting more aggressive targets. Table 6.10 shows how to add measurements to your balanced scorecard.

Table 6.10 Adding measurements and targets to the balanced scorecard

Perspectives	Objectives	Measurements	Targets 2002	2003
Financial	Maximum returns	Return on equity	12%	13%
	Utilization of assets	Utilization rates	7%	8%
	Revenue growth	% change in revenues	+11%	+11%
Customer	Customer retention	Retention %	75%	75%
	Customer service	Survey rating	85%	88%
	Customer relations	% self-initiated calls	35%	40%
Internal processes	Fast delivery	Turnaround time	15m	14m
	Effective service	Problem resolution	68%	69%
	Optimal cost	% cost of sales	66%	64%
	Resource utilization	Productivity indicator	77%	80%
Learning and growth	High skill levels	Skill set ratio	65%	68%
	Employee satisfaction	Survey index	75%	77%
	Outstanding leaders	Five-point ranking	4.5	4.8

Finishing off your balanced scorecard

The final development step is to close the loop and put specific programmes in place to make everything happen. This is the fun part in the entire process. How do we actually hit these targets and meet our strategic objectives? What major initiatives must the organization undertake to make all of this happen? Programmes are the projects that facilitate the execution of everything downstream within the scorecard. Some examples of typical programmes include quality improvement programmes, marketing initiatives, enterprise resource planning (ERP), customer relations management (CRM) and supply chain management.

Programmes usually have certain characteristics. They may:

- be company-sponsored;

- involve designated leaders and cross-functional teams;

- have defined deliverables with milestones along the way;

- have start and stop dates;

- require the allocation of resources, including a budget.

Once programmes have been established and sold to various stakeholders, they tend to add some degree of strategic value or impact. However, getting a major programme launched can be difficult due to funding, apprehension, politics and other obstacles. If existing programmes lose funding, then you need to work back through your scorecard, adjusting your targets and making sure everything still fits.

One of the most important steps in selecting programmes is to plot programmes against all strategic objectives and assess the strategic impact. This can be extremely important since executive management will routinely demand cost reductions during the year. You don't want to cut programmes with the biggest strategic impact. This would undercut your ability to meet strategic objectives. Programmes with little or no strategic impact should get lowest priority within the organization (see Table 6.11).

Table 6.11 Strategic objectives

- Maximum return on equity
- Positive economic value-added
- 15% revenue growth
- 5% reduction in production cost
- Secure 1% market share in Asia
- Obtain competitive pricing
- Develop new market partnerships
- Integrate service process with customer
- Improve production workflows
- Flawless manufacturing
- Expand knowledge distribution
- Link processes to customer inputs
- Engage workforce in the business
- Expand leadership capacities
- Become a customer-driven culture

One of the most common tools used for building balanced scorecards is the template (Table 6.12). Templates are usually spreadsheets, organized to capture, compare and report data used in constructing the balanced scorecard (see Table 6.13 for summary of

Phase II). They represent very basic templates for organizing the data that makes up our balanced scorecard. As with any major project, it is best to deploy three teams for each of these organizational levels:

Table 6.12 Supplement the balanced scorecard with programmes

Objectives	Measurements	Targets 2000	Targets 2001	Programmes
Maximum returns	Return on equity	12%	13%	
Utilization of assets	Utilization rates	7%	8%	
Revenue growth	% change in revenues	+11%	+11%	
Customer retention	Retention %	75%	75%	Customer relations management (CRM)
Customer service	Survey rating	85%	88%	Customer relations management (CRM)
Customer relations	% self-initiated calls	35%	40%	Customer relations management (CRM)
Fast delivery	Turnaround time	15m	14m	Cycle process system
Effective service	First-time resolution	68%	69%	Customer relations management (CRM)
Optimal cost	% cost of sales	66%	64%	Cycle process system
Resource utilization	Productivity indicator	77%	80%	Cycle process system
High skill levels	Skill set ratio	65%	68%	Training system
Employee satisfaction	Survey index	75%	77%	Quality time initiative
Outstanding leadership	5 point ranking	4.5	4.8	Special training programme

Table 6.13 Summary of Phase II

Three major milestones – Phase II
1st   Build measurements for strategic objectives.
2nd   Set targets for each measurement.
3rd   Align programmes with strategic objectives.

- *Leadership team.* Consists of executive management. These are the primary users of the balanced scorecard. Additionally, this is where strategic planning takes place. The leadership team will work closely with the core team in approving the final balanced scorecard. This is where critical decisions are made regarding all aspects of the balanced scorecard.

- *Core team.* Consists of middle-level managers who have a good sense of the overall business. They also understand strategy and work well with members of the leadership team. The core team is responsible for actually building the balanced scorecard, including the strategic maps. The core team works collaboratively with other areas to develop a final balanced scorecard.

- *Measurement team.* Functional area personnel who understand the details and how to get the right kind of information for populating the balanced scorecard. Members of the measurement team typically play no role in strategic planning. They usually have high levels of expertise in a single area of the business. They assist the core team in building certain components of the balanced scorecard, primarily the specific measurements and targets of the scorecard. See Table 6.14.

Table 6.14 Balanced scorecard development

Leadership team	Core team	Measurement team
Sponsors the balanced scorecard, approves the final scorecard, and advocates the concept to other parts of the organization.	Manages the overall project, builds the scorecard, coordinates the process with the leadership and measurement teams.	Delivers critical data such as the measurements that will be used within the balanced scorecard.

Cascading is the process by which you roll out balanced scorecards to different parts of the organization. Since strategizing takes place at the upper level of the organization, one place to start building the balanced scorecard is at the corporate level. Once again, we can go back to our four to five rule: build your scorecard at the upper layer of the organization (corporate); work your way down to the second layer (operating); then work your way down to shared service departments; next, work your way down to the lowest levels such as departments, teams and individuals. By following this process, you can ensure alignment.

Balanced scorecards often require continuous testing and modification to see if the technique really fits. This can be frustrating for executives who routinely expect perfect solutions straight away. Keep in mind that you are testing something that has never been applied before and you must revisit the construction of your scorecard, adjusting and realigning it to fit with your organization. It is not unusual to postpone the roll out of additional scorecards for a year until the first scorecard is well established and working. Therefore, companies that have been successful with the balanced scorecard have a high tolerance for making change happen in a positive way. For example, linking part of employee compensation to the balanced scorecard should be postponed until such time as you have the correct set of measurements in place.

Developing metrics for your organization's balanced scorecard

Your measurement system should consist of the categories shown below:

- *Measuring financial performance.* A good set of metrics to measure past, present and future. It's difficult to develop good metrics for evaluating the future. Some companies have developed economic value-added (EVA) as a single metric that works well to measure company performance.

- *Measuring product and service quality.* You need to choose internal metrics that tell your organization that they have quality products before they deliver them.

- *Measuring supplier performance.* Today outsourcing is a major trend in organizations. If it's not a core competency of the organization then it's cheaper to hire someone else to do it.

- *Measuring customer satisfaction and value.* This is a major weakness in many companies' scorecards. The best way to have a successful customer satisfaction measurement system is to have a balance of data on customer opinions and buying behaviour. The soft data is the opinions. The hard data on buying behaviour lets you know if there is a connection between what customers say and what they actually do. Another important measurement is customer value. Customer value is the ratio of satisfaction over perception of the fairness of price. If I pay a lot of money for a special meal and am extremely satisfied with the food and service but still feel ripped off, I probably won't return. Perceived value is as important as satisfaction, and has to be included in our overall measurement on our scorecard.

- *Measuring processes and operational performance.* It's important not just to focus on measuring output but to develop metrics to measure work in-process. Measuring work activity as it is occurring is using metrics in a preventative fashion.

- *Measuring employee satisfaction.* This is probably the weakest of all the measurements in most organizations' scorecards. Tracking turnover or an annual survey of employees is not enough to evaluate employee morale or satisfaction. Very few people would argue with you about the importance of this metric. However, very few organizations have worked out how best to measure this very important characteristic.

- *Measuring financial performance.* This is the easiest area to measure, because we have so much data on finances.

    - *Yesterday, today and tomorrow financial data.* Yesterday data – this data includes past profits, stock prices and sales. Today data – this is a good measurement of an organizations overall health. Tomorrow data – this strategic data focuses on long-term effects on the company.

- *Economic value-added (EVA)*. Economic value-added is an accurate way to measure organizational profitability. It is more accurate than traditional methods because it includes the cost of capital. EVA is operating profit minus taxes minus the cost of capital.

- *Market value-added (MVA)*. This may be one of the best statistics for indicating the organization's ability to create wealth for shareholders. MVA is a ratio. The top half of the ratio is the capital the company has invested since it began. The bottom of the ratio is the market value of all the company's equity and debt.

- *Activity-based costing (ABC).* Just as EVA is a new way of looking at past financial performance, activity-based costing (ABC) is a new method for calculating the real costs of doing business on a daily basis. ABC is similar to EVA; both are accurate ways of measuring true financial performance. ABC is a method for tracking all costs associated with producing a good or service, not just those costs included in traditional accounting methods. The real value of the ABC approach is in how it allocates costs to specific activities or process steps, rather than to the traditional accounting categories. Traditional cost accounting categories are too broad to be of much use in reducing costs or in diagnosing problems.

- *Cost of quality.* The cost of quality (COQ) is a statistic used today by many organizations to track the amount of labour and materials that is expended on rework or correcting problems. Often, organizations are amazed when they see the true cost of rework. In fact, one German maker of luxury cars found that enough rework went into each of its cars in labour and material to build an entire Toyota Camry from scratch!

Measuring customer satisfaction and value

How do you figure what customers want? You can start with the basics – good quality at a fair price.

- *Determining customer requirements (hot buttons)*. When dealing with customers, it's very important to determine what biases or special requirements they have. In other words, what are their 'hot buttons'?

- *The right way to use scales to measure customer satisfaction*. You need a balance of hard and soft data. Soft measures are customer opinions, perceptions and feelings. Hard data is customer satisfaction – how many customers you gain or lose.

- *A satisfied customer buys from you: a delighted customer sells for you*. A delighted customer is a customer for life. A satisfied customer has very little commitment to the company and would buy from a competitor at any time.

- *The customer satisfaction index (CSI)*. Once you have several good hard (satisfaction) and soft (opinions) customer measures, then you can aggregate them into a single CSI metric. This way, managers can look at this metric to see whether the organization is satisfying customers.

- *Measuring internal customer satisfaction.* This is like a subset of the CSI above. Internal support functions have three major types of customers:

    1. *Users* – employees in other functions who use the products or services produced by the support functions.

    2. *Stakeholders* – shareholders, bosses, corporate executives and others who care about the overall health of the organization.

    3. *Others like us* – business unit or location support function personnel who provide similar products.

- *Linking customer value to customer satisfaction.* It would be beneficial to have two metrics in your scorecard: the customer satisfaction index (CSI) which includes hard and soft measures of customer satisfaction, and a customer value index (CVI). The CVI includes soft or opinion measures on value versus price. Both CVI and CSI work best on a 100-point index with the results weighted as percentages. Some companies combine the CSI and CVI into one metric.

Measuring product and service quality

- *What's the business of your organization – products or services, or both?* This section on your scorecard is where you plot key quality variables relating to the products you manufacture or the services you sell. The input to the data produced comes from tests, inspections and other measurements.

- *Customer requirements drive product and services quality measures.* Feedback from customers will have an impact on future products.

- *Simple formula for success is: attention to detail.* If a person stays one night at a Ritz-Carlton hotel and requests something like a non-feather pillow and non-allergenic face soap, then no matter what Ritz they next stay at, when they arrive and check in those items will be in their room. The Ritz-Carlton maintains an extensive database on its customers.

- *Breaking down products and services and identifying measures.* Complicated or simple products need to be broken down and measured for quality. A complicated product like an aeroplane or a simple product like a tube of toothpaste needs to be measured for important characteristics.

- *What is quality really?* Five measures of quality are: accuracy, completeness, conformance, innovation/novelty and class.

    Now let's try to define those terms. Accuracy and completeness are common terms. Accuracy is synonymous with precision. Completeness is whether all the checklists and walk-throughs are complete. Conformance has to do with whether the product or service meets specifications or standards. It also has to do with whether the product or service looks and performs the way it is supposed to perform. Innovation and novelty are very important for certain types of products and services, and relate to creativity in producing products and services.

- *How to build a product/service quality report card.* Each part of the product/service is given a weight based on its importance to the customer, then each product or service is given a weight based on its sales or importance, to provide a measure of overall quality.

Measuring processes and operational performance

- *Process versus output measures.* The key to excellence in any organization is to control your processes to produce reliable and consistent products and services. The major challenge lies in selecting the right processes to measure. Process and operational measures are more short-term focused.

- *Selecting the right process measure.* The reasons for process measures are that if you control your process you will get the same outputs, time and again.

- *Don't be a copycat!* Many businesses make the mistake of trying to copy the successes of other similar companies. It's better to spend money researching what the customer wants, to come up with a new product offering.

- *Cycle time.* Cycle time is the time that elapses from a customer need being expressed and being satisfied.

- *Employee productivity.* Productivity is a ratio of different types of output to some measure of resources (for example, flights per day/dollars in sales).

- *Safety metrics.* Every company and organization needs to have good safety measures. What you need is a metric to measure some of the outputs and some of the preventative activities.

- *Develop a process scorecard.* I recommend building a simple scorecard using four process measures: productivity, cycle time, safety index and rework index.

Measuring supplier performance

Most companies and organizations now outsource the majority of their non-core processes. Also, many organizations spend a lot of money on goods and services from outside suppliers. This section will give an overview of some of the key mistakes companies make in this area, and provide better ways of tracking the performance of your suppliers.

- *How to change your beliefs and values regarding suppliers.* Many organizations distrust their suppliers. The negative part of this relationship is that it is based on a lack of trust for its own employees. It is important that cooperation and team relationships are built to bridge this distrust gap.

- *How many organizations measure supplier performance?* Many small companies cannot afford to measure supplier performance, and many large companies waste a lot of effort measuring useless data.

- *How to measure customer satisfaction.* This is the part of the supplier's report card that you rate them on how well they performed for you. Some of the dimensions you will want to rate your suppliers on are responsiveness, flexibility, attention to detail, ease of doing business, courteousness of staff and follow-through.

- *Measuring price/value.* If the service is free with the purchase, then the price isn't important. You have at least one hard measure of price so you can measure how the supplier's product or service is different from that of other competitors.

- *Measuring key process variables.* The previous discussion has centred on measuring the supplier's past performance. What's needed now is a way to evaluate the supplier's report card on process or preventative measures that would help the customer and supplier anticipate problems in future. An example of process measures for selling might include number of leads/contacts made with potential new customers.

- *Linking supplier performance measures to key business.* Most organizations make the same mistakes when measuring supplier performance. They tend to measure those things that are easy to measure and fail to link them to the key success factors. You need to develop different report cards. One way to make them different is to assign different weights based on the different products or services the supplier provides. Assigning importance weights to supplier measures allows you the flexibility of having a generic supplier report card format that focuses on the four areas of (1) product/service quality, (2) customer satisfaction, (3) price/value, and (4) process performance. This is a flexible approach which allows you to tailor your report card to each supplier.

Measuring employee satisfaction

In this era of downsizing it's a foreign concept to many companies that their employees are more important than their customers. Many companies are realizing that good business practices will show how well they take care of their employees and will help to determine how they compete in the marketplace.

- *How many companies treat their employees.* In a recent needs assessment, I found out that many employees leave their jobs more because of a lack of a challenge than too little pay. You can delight your customers, delight your employees and make money all at the same time. A satisfied employee will leave for more money or better benefits but a delighted employee will stay and recruit others to join them. If you do nothing else, at least do an annual survey of employee morale.

- *Other ways of measuring the soft measures (opinions and feelings) of employee satisfaction.* As stated above, the soft measures are always opinions and feelings. And the reason these are considered soft is that they change frequently. A way of getting additional clarification on the results of the surveys is to hold employee focus groups. Another way to get employee feedback is to use employee complaints or grievances constructively.

- *Hard measures of employee satisfaction.* Several good hard measures for your scorecard are voluntary turnover, transfer requests, absenteeism and safety.

How to design your own measurement system

Redesigning your own measurement system will save your company money in the long run. There are two main ways of doing this: the top-down and the business unit approach.

The top-down approach

The top-down approach is when an organization, because of its culture, develops a standard set of nine key metrics: return on equity (ROE); earnings growth; capital reinvestment rate; lost-time incidents; compliance with responsible care codes; customer satisfaction; percentage of international sales; percentage of sales from new products; training hours/employee; and employee morale/satisfaction.

The business unit or location-level approach

This approach works for an organization which gives its business units or locations a lot of autonomy.

Step 1: Forming the project team and getting it trained

The first step is to form a cross-section team. It needs to have individuals with standing in the company who are aware of the big picture and what they are working towards. The person who heads up the redesign team of six to eight people is the key player and must have substantial knowledge of the company. To redesign your measurement system: prepare guiding documents, conduct a situation analysis, define key success factors and business fundamentals, identify macro performance measures, develop a measurement plan, design data collection instruments and procedures.

Step 2: Prepare guiding documents

This is the part where you prepare your mission, vision and values statements. I define mission as who you are – your products, services, customers/markets and overall strengths. The definition of vision identifies where you want the organization to be in the future. Values are words or phrases that outline what the company believes in or considers important in running the business.

Step 3: Conduct situation analysis

Situation analysis is usually done as part of the strategic plan. This is not a brainstorming exercise, but requires diligent research. It must be based on facts, not opinions. A situation analysis requires that you assess your strengths and weaknesses and identify trends that will affect your business in the next five to seven years.

Step 4: Define key success factors

This is probably the most difficult and most important step in the process of designing your own measurement system. If you do a poor job of defining key success factors, your measurement system is doomed to failure, and perhaps so is your organization. I start by explaining what key success factors are: defect-free products; a highly skilled and motivated workforce; flexibility to adapt to changing market conditions; continued growth through new product development; delighting customers; partnerships with high-quality suppliers; world-class safety record. The list above is generic; however, most companies would be doing these things if they wanted to be successful. Your key success factors should answer this question: what do you need to do in your business to differentiate yourself from your direct competitors?

Step 5: Identifying key macro performance measures

Team members begin this process by reviewing the key performance metrics. One organization I consulted with whittled its key measures down to 64. This is far too many metrics and requires you to throw them out or revise them into a much smaller number. The three process steps in this phase are: identify measurement categories; brainstorm measures within each category; narrow down measures to the vital few.

Step 6: Identify measurement categories

In Kaplan and Norton's balanced scorecard, they list four boxes or categories: customer, financial, internal and growth/innovation. The customer box includes a variety of hard measures (repeat business/on-time delivery) and soft measures (customer satisfaction). The financial measures are profit, ROI, ROE and sales. Internal measures must be controlled to get good customer performance, financial and growth/innovation measures. Growth and innovation measures deal with things that will impact the company's future.

Step 7: Brainstorm measures within each category

The team members call out possible metrics in response to the four to eight measurement categories. When you finish, you probably will have about 20 metrics in each category. These should be tied in to key success factors. It is important to refer to the key success factors when brainstorming measures, because they all must have at least one associated metric in the final scorecard. Measures on your scorecard also come from considering business fundamentals like market share, growth and meeting regulatory standards.

Step 8: Narrow down measures to the vital few

This third step is to take the 15–20 metrics in each category and narrow them down to three to four. One of the ways to do this is to combine measures in an index. A second way is to eliminate those that are subsets of others. A third method is simply to have team members list their top four metrics in each category.

Step 9: Develop a measurement plan

The next task is to develop a measurement plan. The key success factors and business fundamentals are each assigned numbers. The measures are listed along the left side of the chart. The next column is used to show the data collection method. Some data collection methods listed are surveys, checklists, inspections, analysis, purchase from outside sources, observation, focus groups, laboratory testing, mystery shopper and counting. The third column lists the frequency with which the data is collected. The owner column is optional. But the link to the fundamental or key success factor column is very important. All key success factors need to have at least one associated measure in your scorecard. However, some measures may not be directly linked to a key success factor.

I estimate that it will take between six months and a year to complete the project. Each team member will attend about six half-day meetings and another six two-hour meetings during the project, so this totals about 36 hours per person.

Mission statements and vision statements

This section will deal with mission and vision statements. Basically, the mission statement says who we are; the vision statement says who we want to be. Here is some of the jargon you see in these statements: world-class, competitive, real needs of customers, benchmark level, integrate, innovative, profitable, cost-effective, value-added, targeted customers, customer-focused and market-driven. Most employees I surveyed at one company believed that the mission and vision did not drive performance and that management behaviour was inconsistent with company values.

- *Why mission and vision statements don't work.* Developing mission and vision statements will do nothing to change or improve your organization unless other changes follow. One problem is that employees fail to understand how the company mission and vision relate to their jobs.

- *Developing strategy.* The key to having a good measurement system is to have a good strategy. Measures need to be derived from your strategy and from an analysis of the key business factors you need to concentrate on to ensure that you achieve your vision. Every successful company has a well thought-out strategy. A strategy is how you are going to provide some product or service in such a way that customers would rather deal with your company than with your competitors.

- *The key to a sound strategy.* The key to a sound business strategy is to do something that others cannot do, or do something well that others do poorly.

- *Linking vision, goals, strategies and measures.* Strategy comes out of your vision. Your vision should say where you want to be in five or ten years. Your strategy should articulate in general terms how you will achieve your vision. Once you have identified your vision and key strategies or goals, you need to define key success factors. These are things that will need to happen for you to realize your vision and goals or strategies. Out of your goals, strategies and vision come your performance measures.

Key success factors

Key success factors are things you need to do to achieve your goals and vision. Key success factors relate to the following company goals: competitive pricing, technical capabilities, growing market share, improving profits, investing in new equipment, customized offerings, new products/services, capacity, improving quality, controlling supplier quality, reducing new product development time and targeted marketing.

- *Deriving measures from goals and success factors.* To have a sound measurement system, your measures, goals and key success factors need to be linked. Whatever you have identified as a critical factor for your long-term success should be covered in your overall scorecard.

- *Deceiving measures.* Linking measures to key success factors seems rather simplistic, and it seems unlikely that even a moderately successful business would not have done this. The trick is in making sure that the measures you select are predictive of your ability to achieve your vision and goals. Sometimes your success measures conflict with your vision and goals.

- *Measures and values.* Linking measures with business strategy and goals is not nearly as difficult as making sure that the measures are consistent with your organization's stated values. Values are just as important as having a clear vision. Organizations that truly want to live by their values have found ways of measuring their progress toward this. Values are soft and fuzzy; performance measures are usually hard and quantifiable. So, how do companies ensure that their performance measures and goals don't ignore their values? They do so through the use of a balanced approach to measurement.

Reporting and analysing performance data

Fixing your measurement system will not be a simple task. It will take time and multiple measurement attempts to elevate your company to world-class status.

What's important when reviewing data

Three dimensions are important when reviewing your data. They are level, trend and variability. Level relates to how good your recent performance is when compared with goals, past performance, competitors' performance and benchmark organization. For evaluating, you will need a lot of comparative data. The main question to ask is: 'How well are we doing compared to our goals for last month, year, our competitors and other world-class companies?' Trend is an important dimension because you are looking at multiple data points over time. Trend analysis will reveal whether your performance is either improving, getting worst or static. You will need to have at least seven data points to validate a trend. Variability has to do with fluctuations in trends and levels of performance over time. Variability will answer the question, 'What happened to our performance during the week of August 15th; why did our productivity drop so severely?'

Common problems with data reporting approaches

- *Data is reported in tables rather than graphs.* The whole point of this section can be summarized in one sentence: a graph is always the best way of presenting data. Graphs also typically provide information on levels, trends and variability, information more difficult to pull out of a table of statistics.

- *No comparative data is presented.* It seems that many organizations report data without any comparative statistics or goals. I recommend that you place or draw the goal right next to the graph. Data without goals or something to compare it with is meaningless.

- *Only the most recent data is reported.* You have to look at data several times or you won't pick up the trends.

- *Data is reported unnecessarily.* Most performance reports in the business world are very thick. At the very most, a report should be no longer than 20 pages.

Open-book management: teaching employees to understand performance measures

Open-book management is an approach where companies show and teach their employees how to understand financial information. By doing so, it makes every employee just as concerned as the managers with improving productivity and profitability. One company I worked with devised games to take the difficulty out of financial information.

Understanding the relationships among the measures of your scorecard

The most advanced companies today cannot only tell you what it means when the performance on one of their key metrics changes; they can tell you exactly how performance on one measure impacts on performance on others. To make good and sound business decisions, these types of relationship must be understood.

The big balancing act

Running a business is a juggling act and requires you to build a balanced set of metrics on your scorecard. You need to balance and analyse data early to spot problems before they happen.

Many companies use different words for goals. Here, I am using the word goal to mean the measurable, desired level of performance for a particular measure. A goal always has two parts: (1) the measure itself and (2) the desired level of performance. Some example goals are: reduce voluntary turnover to a level of 7 per cent per year; achieve a score of 98/100 on the annual safety audit; reduce product defects to 30 per 10,000; ninety per cent of our customers will rate their satisfaction with our service as 5 on a 5-point scale. In the first example above, the measure is voluntary turnover and the desired level of performance is 7 per cent; and so on with the other examples. Goals should be set at each level in the organization so that achievement at a lower level leads to achievement at a higher level. One of the problems with goals at lower levels is they tend to be based on projects and activities. It is important to link the process or activity goals to the macro output goals.

Mistakes organizations make when setting goals

The five most common problems with goals are as follows: goals that are really projects, activities or strategies; goals that are based solely on past performance; arbitrary stretch goals; inconsistent short- and longer-term goals; and inconsistencies in goals at different levels of the organization.

- *Goals that are really projects, activities or strategies.* This is the most common error I find in organizations' strategic business plans. The goal should set out the level of performance you want to see on a particular measure. It should not specify how you would achieve this level of performance. The easiest way of making sure that your goals are not strategies or projects is to make sure that each one specifies one of the key measures in your scorecard.

- *Goals that are based solely on past performance.* This mistake occurs when companies assign a goal based on how they did last year. The problem with setting goals based on past performance is that you can delude yourself into believing this is good enough for future performance. Past performance may be helpful when setting goals for the future, but it should not be your only goal.

- *Arbitrary stretch goals.* Today, many companies are setting what are called stretch goals. These are goals that require employees to rethink and re-engineer work. They can eliminate bureaucracy. But I caution that there is a smart way and a foolish way to set stretch goals. To just arbitrarily pick a number and establish it as a goal is the foolish way. This is easy to spot because they are typical round numbers like 10 or 100. Good examples of overall goals are '80 in 5' or Motorola's Six Sigma. The 80 in 5 means that the company would like to see 80 per cent improvement in five years' time. The Six Sigma represents 3.4 defects per million. This was not an arbitrary goal. Motorola carried out detailed researched based on capabilities, past performance and the performance levels of key competitors. These types of goals are not what I would like to see. Goals need to be based on past performance; competitor performance; performance of benchmark-level companies in similar businesses; analysis of technical capabilities and resource constraints; evidence that achievement of the goal/level will make the organization more competitive; feedback from employees and suppliers involved with the goal; and analysis of how goal achievement may impact other measures.

- *Inconsistent short- and longer-term goals.* When I evaluate companies I look for inconsistencies between their annual business plans and their longer-term plans. Annual goals should be based on exactly the same measures as longer-term goals. The annual goal should be a stepping stone to help reach the longer-term goal.

- *Inconsistencies in goals at different levels of the organization.* A similar but different problem with organizational goals is that there are many disconnects across different functions and levels in the organization. Business units typically develop their goals in isolation from other business units doing similar things.

Developing strategies to achieve your goals

Setting goals is easy. What's tough is getting everyone to buy into them. What you need to do is have the person who owns the performance measure to form a group of people to help develop strategies to reach the goal. Next, reduce the list down to a reasonable number of strategies, like three or four. Write a separate project plan for each strategy that specifies deliverables and steps to complete it.

Using benchmarking to improve your strategies

I consider benchmarking to be one of the best methods of establishing realistic stretch goals and getting ideas to achieve those goals. Many companies don't do it right. Taking employees on a field trip around a benchmark company won't leave you with any useful data. What it really takes is multiple phone calls, multiple sources of data and a lot of investigation. You also need to evaluate your culture and the benchmark culture to be sure they are compatible.

Communicating your plan

It's important that all employees know the strategic business plan. If your employees don't know your goals, they won't be able to help you reach them. They need to know the major performance measures, the goals of the organization and the major strategies that will be used to achieve the goals. They also need to know how their functions and jobs will fit in with the organization's goals. Every employee should be able to explain how his performance measures relate to those of the overall company. The key to the effectiveness of the organization is its communication (i.e. the strategic business plan) and how much of it is personal – one on one between employee and supervisor or peer-level employees.

A summary of the key to successful plans

Here are some rules for making your plans effective:

1. Develop specific goals for each performance measure in your scorecard.

2. Identify annual and longer-term goals on the same measures.

3. Set stretch goals that are based on benchmarks and analysis of key competitors.

4. Make sure that goals are consistent across levels and functions.

5. Involve customers, key suppliers and employees in the planning process.

6. Spend no more than six weeks each year preparing your plan; strive for no more than three drafts of the plan document.

7. Employ a systematic approach to select the best strategies to accomplish your goals.

8. Use benchmarking to identify effective strategies for achieving your goals.

9. Communicate plans to all employees using a variety of methods and media, with more reliance on one-on-one communication than on presentations.

In the past, many components for implementing a strategic plan have been managed separately, not collectively within one overall management system. As a result, everything has moved in different directions, leading to poor execution of the strategic plan. Imagine numerous ships all moving in different directions. Imagine these ships are different business units within your organization. You must get all ships moving in the same general direction if you expect to reach your destination (strategic goals).

CHAPTER 7

Your marketing plan

When describing the industry, the present outlook as well as future possibilities should be discussed. You should also provide information on all the various markets within the industry, including any new products or developments that will benefit or adversely affect your business. Base all your observations on reliable data, and be sure to cite sources of information as appropriate. This is important if you are seeking funding; the lender or investor will want to know just how dependable your information is and will not risk money on assumptions.

Marketing

Clearly, without adequate sales, your business cannot survive. The purpose of market research is to provide relevant data that will help solve the marketing problems a business will encounter. This is absolutely necessary in the start-up phase. Your market research and marketing plan form the basis of your projections and are critical to your plan.

The development of market strategies is the result of meticulous market analysis. Conducting market analysis forces the entrepreneur to become familiar with all aspects of his market so that the target market can be defined and the company can be positioned in order to acquire its share of sales.

Not only will market analysis define the market and its sales potential, but it will also enable the entrepreneur to establish pricing, distribution and sales strategies that will allow the business to become profitable within a competitive environment. Market analysis will also provide an indication of the growth potential which will allow you to develop your own estimates for the future of your business.

When conducting marketing research, the process can be broken down into specific stages:

1. Determine the problems that *must* be solved. Properly define the problems by making a list of possible items that will adversely affect the operation of your business.

2. Do those problems require research in order to solve them?

3. List your goals and objectives.

4. Identify the type of data that needs to be gathered to meet those goals. The data could consist of information on customers, competition and the industry.

5. Define the sample audience that will best provide you with the data required.

6. Conduct your market research and gather the information. This could include research tools such as printed material, personal interviews, telephone and mail surveys or sample test marketing.

7. Analyse the data.

8. Finally, develop a conclusion based on the information gathered and determine a course of action. For a profitability improvement plan, your conclusions will generate marketing strategies, key assets that will build entry barriers, and operational and management plans.

Market definition

Begin your market analysis by first defining the market in terms of size, structure, growth prospects, trends and sales potential. Once the size of the market has been determined, the next step is to define the target market. What geographic area will you be targeting primarily? What dollar volume does this market area provide, and what is its growth potential over the next five years? What market share do you expect to capture and why? Who are your main customers – men, women? What age group(s)? What socio-economic group(s)? How important is location to your business? Are you well located to access the market identified? What are the strengths and weaknesses of your location? Who is your competition? What is their competitive strength? Why will customers buy your product or service rather than those of your competition? What is the likely reaction of your competitors to your entry into the marketplace or expansion of your current operation? How do your service and warranty provisions compare to those of the competition? How will the product reach the end user? Distribution includes the entire process of moving the product or service to the customer. Ask yourself these questions: What channels will you use to distribute your product or service? How will you time your distribution? What are your prices, by product line? How did you establish your pricing policy? Are you matching prices with those of your competitors, or are you the one who sets the price in your area? How sensitive are your clients to pricing changes?

Before you can begin developing a pricing strategy, you must first determine the projected costs of running your business. You must add fixed costs, such as property/equipment leases, loan repayments, management cost, salaried employees and depreciation to the variable costs of raw material, inventory, utilities and hourly wages. You must also calculate the cost generated by markdowns, shortages, damaged merchandise, employee discounts, cost of goods sold and desired profits, and add them to the operating expenses listed above to come to an initial price for your product. Ask yourself these questions:

1. What are your pricing objectives?

2. What will be your basic per unit cost of acquisition?

3. Will you offer a discount policy?

4. What will be your per unit price?

5. What do you project your revenue and profit to be?

What is a marketing plan?

A marketing plan is a written statement of how you intend to direct your activity's operations and promote its functions. A marketing plan can be compared to a terrain map. Both will answer three very important questions:

- What is your present situation? (Where does your activity fit in the competitive market?)

- Which direction did you come from? (Has your activity been doing the right things in the past?)

- Which direction should you go? (What things should your activity be doing to ensure success?)

There are five main sections in a marketing plan. The first section, the executive summary, is a brief summary of the entire marketing plan. Its purpose is to give the reader quick information without him having to read the entire report.

The middle three sections – the external environment analysis, the needs assessment and the organizational assessment – serve as your information storehouse or database. Planning must be based upon facts, and your planning and decision-making will rest upon this firm foundation of data. Now let's take a closer look at each of these three sections.

The external environment analysis will help you examine the setting in which your activity operates. You'll uncover specific information about how well or how poorly your competition is doing in the marketplace. You'll also collect valuable information on the economic, social and technological aspects of your activity's operating environment. You'll get a thorough understanding of your customers' needs and wants from the needs assessment section. A needs assessment is an organized method of gathering and analysing data about your installation's business community. You can obtain this information by surveying your clients, by working in focus groups with consumers, by holding brainstorming sessions with subject matter experts, or by reviewing previously written (historical) documents on a given subject.

Next, you'll study your activity's internal operating environment (organizational assessment). You'll examine how your activity's operation in the marketplace is affected by its command, its employees, its resources and by the business system in general (especially regulations). Once you've evaluated conditions outside and inside your activity's operating environment and you have a thorough understanding of your community's needs and wants, you'll develop goals and objectives for your activity (organizational assessment).

Last, in the strategy development section, you'll describe how your company will carry out its plans for satisfying community needs.

Why a marketing plan is valuable to you

Here are some of the ways that a marketing plan can help your activity:

1. A marketing plan serves as a planning tool. Whether you're developing long-range goals and objectives for your activity or planning a new programme or product, a marketing plan will

make your job easier. How? By guiding you through the orderly steps of planning. Think back to the last time you developed or revised a product or programme for your activity. Like most managers, you probably tried very hard to plan for success. You did what you thought should be done. But do you remember having a nagging feeling that maybe you didn't cover all the bases as far as planning was concerned? Few people would feel comfortable building a house without a set of plans; likewise, few people would feel confident in planning for their activity without a guide. When you use a marketing plan, you'll have the assurance of having done a thorough job of planning.

2. A marketing plan helps you determine where your activity fits in the competitive market. Can you say why people should choose your activity instead of one of your competitors? Do you know how your products and your pricing compare to other similar establishments? A marketing plan for your activity will give you a clear picture of your competitive arena. You'll clearly see what your activity should (and should not) be doing in order to best serve the business community.

3. A marketing plan helps you determine which direction your activity came from and which way it should be going. Good planning for the future requires looking back at your activity's past performance, focusing especially on how well it has served its customers. Based upon your understanding of what led to its present operating condition, you'll then be ready to develop goals and objectives for your activity (see strategy development section).

4. A marketing plan serves as your information source for future planning. Let's suppose that you're planning to run some new programmes. Naturally you want to plan them thoroughly. About six months ago, you completed a marketing plan for your activity. Does this mean that you have to develop a whole new marketing plan for the new programmes? No. You don't need to develop a new marketing plan each time you make changes and adjustments in your activity. Why not use the research that you've already done for your marketing plan as the basis for developing these new programmes (or products) for your activity? (Actually, it's best to revise or rewrite your activity's marketing plan annually to keep pace with changing conditions. If conditions change radically during the course of a year, you'll need to develop a new marketing plan.)

Here's another benefit– a marketing plan serves as a touchstone for evaluating your activity's operations. At any point in time, you can look at your activity's performance and compare it to what you projected in your marketing plan. You can tell whether your activity is on target in meeting its goals and objectives.

5. A marketing plan helps you manage your activity's resources. A marketing plan is more than a planning tool – it's a management tool as well. It will help you appraise your activity's resources, its employees, and its strengths and weaknesses. You'll design ways of managing your activity's assets as you move through the strategy development section. With dwindling resources and continued budget cutbacks on the horizon, it's hard to think of a more persuasive tool for justifying your funding requests than

a well-documented marketing plan. A marketing plan puts your activity in a very professional light. By documenting what is working well, what needs fixing and which resources you need in order to maintain or improve a quality product, you'll be in a very convincing position to state your case to your superiors.

6. Your marketing plan will help your activity remain competitive. Most analysts agree that business competition will become even fiercer in the coming decade. Your competitors probably have a well-devised plan for increasing their market share. What will be your activity's response?

Chapter 8 deals with how to develop and write a marketing plan.

CHAPTER 8

Developing a marketing plan

You, as an activity manager, don't have to develop the marketing plan alone. In fact, it's better if you include your staff. Developing your marketing plan in a cooperative effort boosts morale by fostering staff participation. Your staff members will feel a pride of ownership toward the planning strategies that they help develop. Tap into your staff members' wealth of knowledge and expertise.

Executive summary

The executive summary is a brief presentation of the high points of your marketing plan. Write this section after you finish all the others. Consult Step 20 of the guide given later in the chapter.

External environment analysis

Part of the fun of travelling by aeroplane is looking at the country from a bird's-eye view. It's fascinating to see how everything fits together – the roads, the buildings, the scenery. We get a different perspective of our environment; we can see how things fit in an overall scheme. In business, it's also important to get a fresh perspective of things from time to time. The external environment analysis section of your marketing plan will help you do just that. The external environment analysis is a look around at the setting in which your business operates. It paints a picture of your business world – outside the boundaries of your activity. As you complete this section, you'll get a general picture of the major elements that influence your business environment.

It's best to begin your marketing plan with an external environment analysis because it puts things into perspective: that is, it clearly marks the boundaries that your activity works within. Below are some of the major questions that the external environment analysis will answer for you.

- What is the competition doing, and how will it affect your business?

- What is the condition of the economy? How is it affecting your business?

- How is technology affecting your business? What is the state-of-the art technology in your business field?

- How does your business's equipment compare to that of your competitors?

- What legal and political factors are now or will be important to consider in your business's game plan?

- What influence will social and cultural factors have on how you market your product?

- What ecological factors should you consider in planning?

Step 1: Evaluate your competitive environment

Let's begin by sizing up your competition. Your competition is a very important aspect of your external environment.

Your direct competition includes those places where your customers/potential customers can go to obtain the same product that your business offers. Indirect competition includes those places where your customers/potential customers can spend their time or money, although they are not dealing with products that are related to those you offer. For example, suppose you are the manager of a club, and you are planning a dance for Friday evening. Some of your customers may choose other events, such as going to the theatre, going bowling, or just staying at home and watching television. These other events would be indirectly competing with your activity.

Take note of how influential and how extensive the competition is. What sort of competition are you up against? Think in terms of threats and opportunities to your business. For example, any new potential competitor in the marketplace would obviously be a threat to your activity if it has the potential of taking away part of your market share. A competitive threat can come from not only a commercial enterprise, but also from other business – even if it is unrelated to your field of business – merely because you both may be scheduling events for the same times. Also be alert for opportunities to expand your operation, such as a competitor who is closing, relocating or changing its management.

Collect any additional information about your competition that you think is important. You may wish to visit your competitors. Network with other activity managers. Add that information to your worksheets.

Be sure you have determined the following:

- the impact of your competitor on your activity;

- all unique features of the competition's products;

- the relative market share for your activity and your competitors';

- the competition's marketing tactics.

Remember to keep the tone of your writing neutral, much as a reporter would write a newspaper article. Deal in facts; treat the data objectively.

Step 2: Evaluate your local economic environment

As an activity manager, you should be regularly monitoring the state of the local economy. From your general knowledge, jot down some notes. Here are some questions to jog your thinking:

- Is the local economy on the rise or decline?

- In what ways will economic trends affect how your customers and potential customers use your activity?

- If consumer spending is declining, does this mean that your customers will be spending less time or money at your activity?

Think in terms of threats and opportunities.

Step 3: Evaluate your technological environment

Does your business have any competitive advantages from its use of certain equipment or processes? Or is it at a disadvantage because it is lacking in this area? Find out what forms of technology are available that would help you serve the business community better. Try turning as many threats into opportunities as you can.

Consider technology from two aspects:

1. *Product technology.* Is your activity providing goods at the level of development or advancement that your customers require? Suppose, for example, that you are managing an outdoor recreation centre. You would need to determine whether the camping equipment that your activity provided was at the right level of technological development required by your customers. Is it possible that your customers, some of whom are accustomed to military gear, may not be comfortable with equipment that is popular on the civilian market? On the other hand, if your customers are looking for a certain level of product sophistication, then you may have to do some upgrading of your product. Think of ways to match the level of your product technology to your customers' requirements.

2. *Process technology.* Process technology pertains to the ways and means of getting jobs done, such as doing paperwork, keeping

records, providing a service and making sales. Does your business operate using the latest available methods for improving efficiency? Again, suppose you're the outdoor recreation centre manager. Could operational efficiency be improved by using your new computer system to reduce paperwork? Could you train somebody to perform some advanced accounting functions on it, for example?

Step 4: Evaluate your legal/political environment

Like most other aspects of modern living, our political and legal scene is very complicated and is ever-changing. Therefore it's important to keep on top of the legal and political issues that may affect your business.

Review recent national and local political issues, policies and regulations. Sort out those that affect your business. Jot down your thoughts about how recent laws and rulings are affecting your business. This may sound like a tall order, but one way of doing this sort of research is to go to your library and look over the Sunday issues of a newspaper that provides comprehensive coverage of such matters. Look through the table of contents to help jog your memory of past events. Or use a popular weekly news magazine. Go back through the past nine to twelve months. Pick out a few political issues from each. Skim through any of the articles that deal with issues affecting your business. One or two hours' worth of work should do it.

Now go one step further – try to anticipate possible changes in the laws and regulations that may affect your business. Changes could pose either a threat or an opportunity to your business. In what ways would your business need to adjust to those changes (and possibly seize upon some opportunities)?

Step 5: Evaluate your social/cultural environment

All societies change over time. Values are being constantly re-examined. Behavioural patterns and expectations change continuously. Our society today is the result of a long series of changes and modifications.

What social issues do people feel are most important? Is your business capable of meeting these demands? Think in terms of threats and opportunities. For example, consider healthier lifestyles – nearly everyone has now become alert to new ways of thinking about what we eat, how we need to exercise, and the general improvement in how we treat our bodies and minds. Pressure is growing from customers for better foods (e.g. non-genetically modified) and safer environments. This demand for healthier lifestyles might affect your business in negative ways (as threats). If, for example, you're managing a restaurant, you may have to make some changes on the menu or in the way certain foods are prepared. However, this new demand can also affect your business in positive ways (as opportunities). This could be your chance to attract new customers by offering new types of health foods!

Here are some other recent changes in our society for you to consider:

- recent changes in family structure, such as dual income families, single parents, extended (step) families, and the dwindling amount of time available for parents to spend with their children;

- women in the workforce, resulting in higher disposable incomes, changes in the work environment and changes in product demands;

- our society's ageing population, with the resultant increasing demand for social services, decreased emphasis on youth, and more attention to the older segment of the population;

- increased demand for training and education, such as more adults returning to evening classes for better job skills and more sophisticated use of leisure time;

- increased awareness of drug and alcohol abuse, an emphasis on socially responsible behaviour, and demand for alternate activities.

Consider the latest trends in the social environment (both at the national and local levels) that impact your business.

Step 6: Evaluate your ecological environment

Is your business situated in an area that is sensitive to environmental issues? Restrictions and limitations on business activities are increasing rapidly. For example, what plans do you, the arts and crafts centre manager, have for disposing of toxic materials, such as used chemicals and left-over paints? Does your business participate in any recycling programmes? Should you begin one?

Again, look at the threats involved in ecological issues, such as higher operating costs, increased paperwork and perhaps operating under more restricting conditions. Likewise, search out any potential opportunities associated with environmental issues. If your area has very cold winters, for example, could your business provide some service for your community members to help get them through the difficulties and boredom of that season?

Step 7: Determine your customers' needs

What's the purpose of carrying out a needs assessment? A needs assessment will answer two key questions concerning your customers:

1. What do the business community members need or want (as far as my business is concerned)?

2. How can my business help fill these needs?

Does this all sound too difficult to do? Don't stop now! If you're willing to invest a little more energy, your efforts will pay off the rich dividend of knowing that your planning efforts will result in products that the community really needs and wants! Now, how do you do a needs assessment?

First, you decide on the present situations or conditions that need investigation. Perhaps something is not happening... something is wrong... the community is lacking in some area. Maybe you wish to see if your customers' needs have changed over a period of time. Perhaps you feel that one of your products or programmes needs alteration, but you want to find support for making the changes. Or maybe you want to see if your business is doing things right, as a confirmation that you are meeting the community's needs. In other words, there is an information gap that needs to be filled.

Next, choose a method for collecting your information. Will you go directly to your customers by using a survey? Will you use brainstorming sessions or focus groups? Maybe you'll decide that doing historical research is sufficient. After you pick a method for collecting your data, you'll need to plan how to use it. If you choose to use a survey, try it out on a small test group first. A first draft usually needs some revisions. You may wish to practise a focus group or brainstorming session with some of your staff members before holding actual sessions. Try to anticipate some of the responses that you'll get, and practise how to deal with those responses. Then collect the data and analyse it carefully. The object of analysing data is to look for trends or patterns. I suggest categorizing the data into two main parts: the needs or concerns of the respondents and population characteristics.

Quantify your information to help highlight major trends. If you're familiar with using basic statistics, by all means apply them. If not, ask someone who can help you. Now comes the time to present your data findings in your marketing plan. Divide the needs assessment section into two parts. In the first part, briefly describe the method you used to collect the information. Present highlights of the data that you consider most important. Concentrate on the factors that your business can have some control over, given its abilities and constraints. Tabulate the data for easier reading wherever possible. In the second part, give a brief interpretation of the data. Again, stress the issues/concerns that your business is capable of doing something about. Use a positive approach. This doesn't mean that you should give false impressions. If something is wrong, say so. Nevertheless, show the reader how your business can address these issues.

Organizational environment assessment

Let's pause at this point and review what you've accomplished so far. You began by examining your business environment (external environment analysis). This gave you a picture of the setting that your business operates within. Then you took a careful look at your customers' wants and needs (needs assessment). Now, with the organizational assessment, you're ready to work toward developing goals and objectives for your business. Next, you'll take an inventory of your business's strengths and weaknesses. You'll review opportunities for your business to grow and advance in serving the business community. Of course, proper planning also includes addressing the negative factors or threats which will adversely affect your business. Then, after you've assessed your capabilities and limitations, you'll write your goals and objectives.

Let's take this one step at a time. Begin your organizational assessment with a description of your chain of command.

Step 8: Evaluate the impact of your structure

In this part of your marketing plan, you'll give a brief picture of the operating guidelines set by the leadership at your business. Describe their approach to activities, particularly toward your activity. Are they tuned in to important subjects? If not, what could you do to help get more support? (Remember to use an objective tone in your writing.)

What impact does management have on your operation? How does their philosophy relate to yours? Be sure to take into consideration your mission and its impact on your management's philosophy.

Step 9: Evaluate your staff's performance

Take an objective look at your staff. Consider the quality of their work – their attitudes, motivation and general morale. How do these factors affect your customers? Is personnel performance satisfactory? If so, what is needed to maintain that level of performance? If their performance is deficient, what are the root causes – poor motivation, insufficient or inadequate training, negative environmental factors or a combination of these? Remember: the bottom line in your analysis of personnel performance is customer satisfaction!

Step 10: Evaluate your business's resources

What resources does your business have (or require) in order to meet your customers' needs? Divide these resources into three categories: personnel, facility and funds.

1. *Personnel.* Your staff members are your most vital resources. They represent your activity and help distinguish it from the competition. How do your staff affect the quality of customer service? Look at the size of your staff. With today's lean

budgeting, you need to be sure you're utilizing your employees in the most effective ways. Are staff always available at the most critical times? Maybe work schedules need adjusting. Are you thinking about recruiting volunteers? Have you considered commercial sponsorship for special events?

2. *Facility.* Consider the condition, age and location of your facility. What impact does it have on your customers? What kind of message does its appearance send out? Are people attracted to or turned away by its appearance? Are there any hazards, such as peeling paint or stairways, that need repair? Is your business located in a place that's easy to get to? Which factors can you do something about? Are there alternative ways of getting improvements done? If funding is tight, can you think of other ways to raise money for those needed items? Is commercial sponsorship available for the grand opening of your new programme?

3. *Funds.* Be sure to refer to your business's budget and financial statement when addressing funds. Point out the limitations and opportunities that your current funding situation presents for your business.

Step 11: Evaluate your activity's consumers

Your objective for this step is to clearly define your activity's target markets. Who are your customers now? Who should your customers be? Think in terms of primary and secondary target markets. Who are you currently reaching with your marketing efforts (primary target market)? Are there other significant target markets that you're missing (secondary target markets)? Are there secondary target markets that you can satisfy with your current products? Can you offer new or different products to better satisfy your present customers or attract new customers?

Base your decisions mainly upon your needs assessment. Include other factors from your external environment analysis, where applicable. Evaluate your current products and proposed products in terms of the target markets that you have defined.

Step 12: Evaluate the impact of the business's operational structure on your activity

The operational structure analysis provides a snapshot of the organization or product and the situation it currently faces. A brief description of the product, sales, markets currently served, profitability and obstacles facing the marketing effort are outlined here. To determine profitability, you would normally look at your existing costing systems. Often your analysis will be addressing another member of your organization who may know everything you put in your analysis. That's OK. The real purpose of this section is to give you some facts on which to build your marketing strategy. Restating these facts gives you a chance to discover if other members of your team view the situation the same way you do.

Step 13: Do a SWOT analysis for your activity

We've all read books and articles on self-improvement – topics such as how to be more successful, more persuasive, etc. Regardless of the topic, the approach is generally the same. Before we can develop strategies for self-improvement, we must first take a personal inventory of ourselves and find our strengths and weaknesses. For example, let's say your needs assessment showed that your restaurant is very popular. Your patrons enjoy the fine quality of food and service. That's a strength of your activity. Strengths are attributes that your activity possesses which help it serve the business community. Strengths are controllable; you have control over the quality of your activity's operation. Strengths give your activity a competitive edge. Let's say that your needs assessment indicated that your selection of goods is too narrow. That's a weakness, because narrow selection is damaging your operation. You can do something to change that situation, such as increasing the variety of your selection.

Now let's talk about opportunities for your activity. Think of some changes in the external environment that your business could use to better serve its customers. Perhaps there are new products coming on the market that would be beneficial to your customers. Note that opportunities are events that occur in the outside world that you cannot control. However, you can seize opportunities and utilize them to enhance your activity's service.

Finally, let's discuss the major threats that confront your activity. Threats are negative events that are affecting your activity. Like opportunities, threats are uncontrollable. However, you can take steps to lessen their impact. Think of a threat as a hurricane that's coming your way. You can't change its course, but there are some actions you can take to reduce the damage, such as taping your windows and storing extra food and water.

This SWOT (Strengths, Weaknesses, Opportunities, Threats) section of your marketing plan is designed to provide a quick look at your business's capabilities. The key to writing this section is conciseness. Write the SWOT section of your marketing plan using bullets to highlight the main points. As with the rest of your marketing plan, maintain a positive, professional approach to improving or maintaining your activity's operation.

At the beginning of this chapter, I stressed the importance of your staff members having an active role in the development of your marketing plan. This is especially important with regard to analysing your activity's SWOT. Make extra copies of the SWOT worksheets. Explain the concepts we have discussed in this section and heartily encourage staff participation. Staff members are often very capable of appraising the activity that they work in. They get to see and hear things that managers simply cannot due to work relationships and business structure. Don't overlook this critical source of information!

Development of goals and objectives

Up to this point, most of your effort has been devoted to analysing the factors that make your activity what it is. Now you're on your way toward developing your activity's marketing strategies.

Step 14: Cite your mission

Your objective for this section is to show how your activity's marketing strategies will support your business goals. Start with a brief statement of your mission(s). Next, move to your department's mission(s). Show how they support those of the business as a whole. Conclude with a statement of your activity's mission(s). Show how they support the missions of the company and the department.

Step 15: State your activity's goals and objectives

This section is the central point of your marketing plan. So far, you've collected a lot of important background information. Now it's time to describe your plans for your activity and how you intend to accomplish them.

Goals are long-term visions for your activity. They are general descriptions of what your business will look like or what it will be doing in the near future.

Here's what you need to know about objectives:

1. Objectives describe specific actions. They say what action you will take to fulfil a goal. Keep your objectives short. Use action verbs wherever possible. Use nouns that bring clear images and ideas to the reader's mind.

2. Objectives are measurable. They indicate how much change or improvement to expect. Some examples of measurable criteria are increases in customer attendance, increases in revenue and reductions in costs.

   Avoid using specific quantities in your objectives, such as cash amounts, numbers of people and similar measurements. Use percentages as criteria instead. This will allow you more flexibility in adapting to unforeseen events. For example, suppose you project a $10,000 increase in sales for a given quarter. Then something unexpected happens making that cash amount you projected now impossible. However, by using a percentage, your objective would remain viable despite any uncontrollable changes in conditions.

3. Objectives are designed to be accomplished within a given time period. They say when the action will take effect. Develop your objectives with a completion timeline in mind.

Strategy development

Goals are the broad plans for carrying out your business's mission. Your objectives elaborate on what methods you will take to reach your goals. The organizational assessment section of your marketing plan has taken you as far as developing goals and objectives for your business. You still need to plan the details of putting your objectives into action. We'll call these planning details strategies.

Developing strategies means choosing specific courses of action for your business. Address topics such as how your business will gain a larger share of the market, how it will enter new areas of the market or how it will maintain its present level of success.

Step 16: Develop product strategies

Different products consist of different mixtures of qualities or attributes. You'll develop some of your marketing strategies by addressing your product's attributes.

- *Brand name.* The name of your activity is its brand name. Brand name is the first thing that pops into your customers' minds when they think about your product. For example, if someone plans to work on his car, subconsciously your business's name Auto Repair Centre flashes through their minds. They probably aren't even aware that this happens. It happens instantly. And in that instant, either a positive, negative or neutral image will form in your customer's mind.

- *Packaging and labelling.* Packaging applies to goods; labelling applies to goods, services and ideas. Product packaging and labelling also trigger mental images in your customers' minds. For example, where would you rather have lunch – in a café or in a posh restaurant? Packaging and labelling play an important part in how customers regard your products. Some examples of packaging and labelling include your logo (labelling), information brochures (packaging), shopping bags with your activity's name (packaging), and programmes that you hand out at the front door for your activity's seminar on retirement planning (labelling).

- *Guarantees and warranties.* These two items, which are part of both goods and services, usually come in an explicit, written form. One of the most common forms is the service warranty on an appliance. A less obvious form of written guarantee is the promises or pledges that some shops have on their walls that assure customer satisfaction.

Ask yourself, how can our customers be sure that our product's quality will always be high? How consistent is the quality of our products? Consumers will usually have some level of expectations for quality. How does your business meet (or exceed) those expectations?

- *Service.* Service is the way in which your product is delivered to the customer. Service is a critical product attribute. Whether a customer continues to use your product depends largely upon how you offer it. Customers look for personalized treatment, such as helpfulness and friendliness. The importance of good customer service has been proven in many marketing studies.

- *After-sales service.* The key to continued acceptance of your product is the satisfaction of your customers' needs long after the product has been delivered. After-sales service reinforces the initial benefits that your customers receive when they use your business.

- *Special features.* You must continually meet the customer's challenge: 'Why should I use your business when I can just as easily go somewhere else?' This question is especially important regarding your potential customers. What does your activity offer that is special? What distinguishes your product from the competition's?

- *Physical traits.* This attribute applies only to goods. Where applicable, identify your product's physical traits that satisfy your customers' needs. Which attributes are most important to your customers?

- *Safety.* Assure your customers that your product will be physically and, where applicable, psychologically safe (for example, non-threatening, not embarrassing, not stressful). Customers must be comfortable using your product. Be certain to carefully word your statements on product safety and keep them in a positive light.

- *Image*. Be continuously aware of your customers' concept of your activity and its product. Regardless of what you perceive to be the truth about your activity, if your customers begin to form negative impressions, you will eventually lose their business! Look at your activity and its products from your customers' perspective, and then plan your strategies.

- *Other benefits*. Customers will often return not only for direct benefits, but also for such reasons as comradeship or for sharing common career interests. Be alert to the secondary benefits that your activity offers (and can offer), and find ways of highlighting them.

Step 17: Develop pricing strategies

Price includes all expenses – monetary, non-monetary, direct and indirect – that the customer is willing to pay in order to fulfil a desire or need. You need to determine all types of expenses that the consumer is willing to pay for your product in order to develop sound pricing strategies. Usually, the customer pays direct monetary costs when purchasing a product. For example, you may decide to charge $3.00 for each class in computer training. Direct monetary costs are simple. They are the cash amount of the product – and nothing more.

If your marketing plan includes a price change, then discuss both past prices and proposed prices. Include your reason for the change as well. Be sure to consider the indirect monetary costs of your product. These are expenses that the customer pays money for other than the actual price of the product. Consumers may also pay for products in non-monetary terms. Time and effort are among the most common examples. Customers have to spend their valuable time and effort to get your products. Remember: these two resources are very limited! Most people will think twice before trying to fit something else into their busy schedules. When your customers decide to go to your function, they are agreeing to pay the non-monetary costs of time and effort.

Some non-monetary costs are more subtle. Each time a customer purchases your product, she gives up the opportunity to purchase something else. For example, if your customer decides to come to your computer training classes, she cannot go to a football match at the same time. Some non-monetary costs will have a more serious impact, such as those with psychological implications. Be especially aware of the high cost that your customers pay when they participate in programmes or activities that may cause embarrassment, stereotyping or possible impediment to their careers (as with substance abuse programmes, preparation for childbirth classes and other sensitive areas).

How you determine the price for your product will depend mainly on the circumstances within which you operate. You may find that you have complete pricing freedom, limited pricing freedom or no pricing freedom (mandated prices). In any case, you need to carefully consider all the expenses your customers incur when they purchase your products. This will broaden your understanding of your customers and their wants and needs. Your alertness to the various types of customer costs also might help you reduce your customers' indirect monetary and non-monetary expenses. (Naturally, you'll also need to continuously monitor the cost of your goods and how much it costs you to provide your products.)

Which expenses – monetary, non-monetary, direct, indirect – are the most important? That depends on how much you can control your products' pricing. Be sure your business can afford to produce the products that will satisfy the community's needs. Evaluate your budget constraints. If it is not possible for you to do everything, then prioritize the products that are most needed.

Step 18: Develop place strategies

Place strategies include all efforts and resources required to facilitate the flow of goods, services or ideas as they move from the producer to the consumer. Proper place components ensure that your products are where your customers can find them, when they want them.

- *Location.* Your business may have a great location which helps attract customers. In many cases, however, this is not true. Is your location readily accessible to consumers? Does your location tend to keep customers away? Generally, there isn't much you can do about your location. But there are indirect ways you can change or reduce its effects.

- *Plant.* Is the physical plant (i.e. the site, facility, building, furnishings, etc.) attractive to your customers? Does it reflect the image that your business wishes to portray? Look at your layout. Is it conducive to the kind of business that you do? What about furnishings? Atmosphere? Cleanliness? Are these items satisfactory? If so, what will you do to keep these going for you? If your plant has a negative impact... (by now you know what we're going to say!)

- *Inventory.* Do you maintain a sufficient supply of products, supplies and materials to satisfy consumers' requirements? Maybe a more appropriate question is: can you? What are the factors that prevent you from maintaining an adequate supply? Address these factors in your marketing plan whether or not they are controllable.

- *Timing.* Is your product available when your customers want/need it? Are your hours of operation convenient for your customers?

- *Transportation.* Transportation refers to the delivery of your products to a location where your customers can obtain them. Is your product available to your customers where they can readily get it? (Transportation does not refer to your customers having to travel to get to your business.)

Step 19: Develop a promotional mix

Promotion is marketing communication. It is the exchange of information between suppliers and consumers. Promotion is designed to inform, remind and persuade consumers to respond to your product. (Advertising is a form of promotion, that is persuasion.) There are two major facets of a promotional mix. Controllable elements are those in which the business can control the information and its dissemination. Advertising (print, radio, television), contests, personal selling and point-of-purchase displays are examples of controllable elements. Obviously, these elements are the most desirable, but are not always available due to cost, regulatory restrictions or other reasons.

Uncontrollable elements are those where the business cannot control either the information content or its dissemination. Publicity/public relations, referrals and word-of-mouth are common types of uncontrollable elements. They're also very effective!

Writing your marketing plan

All of your research, analysis and planning is now finished. You have completed your marketing research and have done an extensive analysis of your business's position in the marketplace. You have also developed the goals and objectives for your business, along with a strategic action plan for attaining the desired ends. Now you're ready to compile your wealth of information into a formal written record.

Step 20: Develop a written plan

Be sure that your goals and objectives are clearly derived from your external analysis, needs assessment and organizational assessment. In turn, be sure that your strategy development is clearly based on specific goals and objectives. Read over all of your material and look for patterns or trends that you may wish to address. You may have to whittle down some of your data. If so, decide on what is most important and delete the remaining material. Once you feel familiar and comfortable with your data, you're ready to start writing. One of the keys to good writing is getting off to the right start. Sit down in a quiet place and get into a marketing frame of mind. Think about your specific topic (let's say it's external environment analysis). Begin jotting down your preliminary thoughts as fast as they come to you – quickly and briefly. Use bullets. Keep jotting them down while you have the inspiration. Once you've exhausted your thoughts, go back and read them over. Flesh them out a bit with short phrases so they become more coherent. Then organize your bullets into major categories, which will become your paragraphs.

Start writing by addressing each of your bullets. Write with a sense of direction. Beginning with the external environment analysis, go through the stages of research and investigation about your business and its products, toward your business's goals, objectives and strategies.

Once you have established the key assets and skills necessary to be successful in this business and have defined your distinct competitive advantage, you need to communicate them in a strategic form that will attract market share as well as defend it.

1. What will your advertising campaign theme be?

2. What will your copy theme be?

3. What type of media do you plan to use?

4. How frequently will you use these avenues?

5. How big will your adverts be?

6. How much will they cost?

7. What is your advertising budget?

In your marketing plan you should discuss and define how you will set up your advertising campaign, keeping in mind the above questions.

Advertising or other promotion is often very important to the success of a business in its first year of operation. Does your business require a promotion plan? If so, explain the type and amount of promotion you plan to use.

1. What budget will you have to work with?

2. How will you position your product or service?

3. Will your promotions be coordinated with distribution schedules?

4. What are your sales promotion objectives?

5. Will you employ extensive personal selling?

6. How large will your sales staff be?

7. What type of publicity will you seek?

Developing a focused sales strategy

Selling financial services to businesses is a long and complex process. And in competitive markets where the best companies have long-standing relationships with their current supplier, the selling process becomes even more difficult. This presents a problem that most suppliers must address. If a supplier wants to grow its assets or market share without sacrificing asset quality or margins, it must find a way to develop new business with the best businesses in its market. But how does a supplier get these best businesses into its portfolio? By taking them away from a competitor. But taking a good business away from a good competitor is difficult and time consuming. However, it can be done.

New business comes from a combination of two sources: current customers and new customers. A large percentage of any supplier's revenues comes from current customer relationships. Increasing existing facilities, adding facilities and selling additional non-credit services are primary sources of new business for most suppliers. The process of growing existing customer relationships has been thoroughly discussed within the business industry. The process is straightforward: identify the best and the highest potential customers in the portfolio, develop account plans for each of these customers, implement the account plan and then continually monitor the relationship.

Most of this discussion, however, will focus on the second source of new business – new customers – for two important reasons. First, most suppliers still seem to be struggling with new business development. Second, if the process of developing new clients is understood, it's easy to apply that understanding to growing current client relationships. To understand the process of developing new customer relationships, one must understand the buying process. So, before discussing the strategies and methods of new customer development, we need to focus on how a buyer, let's say a business owner, evaluates and buys business products and services. Let's start by establishing a few assumptions.

- *Assumption one.* The business industry is a mature industry; suppliers in a given market generally provide the same kinds of services, in a similar manner, at about the same cost. To the average business owner, the difference between suppliers is minimal. Consequently, he doesn't see a significant difference between one provider of business services and another. In this situation, most business owners have little incentive to change suppliers. And when they go through a period of dissatisfaction with their current supplier, they think, due to their similar perception of all suppliers, that they won't be able to do much better even if they go to the trouble of changing suppliers.

- *Assumption two.* In a mature industry and marketplace, all the good customers are taken. What do we mean by a good customer? A good customer is one who meets a supplier's requirements for asset quality, ROA (or potential ROA) and relationship orientation.

- *Assumption three.* All human relationships change over time. They go through cycles, satisfying at one moment, dissatisfying at another, then satisfying again. Business owners go through the same satisfaction cycles with their suppliers. Few business owners are totally satisfied with their current supplier. Inevitably, they will go through some period of discontent – a period which could last for minutes, days or months.

Let's look at strategies for dealing with these assumptions.

Strategy no. 1: Maintain frequent contact

The objective of this strategy is straightforward: keep your name in front of business owners until they have a need for your business – you want to look at the next piece of business they have.

All relationships go through cycles. Over time a business owner will cycle through periods of increasing and decreasing satisfaction with his current supplier. This fact is a key element in the process of developing new clients. If you were to contact a prospect when he was very dissatisfied (at a low point in the cycle), he may be receptive to your ideas. And, if you were to contact a good prospect only once a year and you happened to catch him in a period of dissatisfaction, you would say your timing was good. If, on the other hand, you caught the prospect during a period of satisfaction, you would say your timing was bad. Given this cyclicality, common sense would tell you that contacting a prospective customer six, eight or ten times in a one-year period would greatly increase the odds of making a contact during a period of dissatisfaction. Therefore, one approach to developing new business is based on timing: maintain contact with a good prospect often enough (several times a year) and long enough (for one, two or three years) until you get lucky and hit a period of dissatisfaction. However, this approach will require three things to be successful:

1. A consistent effort – contacting a small number of prospects again and again rather than calling on a large number of prospects once.

2. A persistent effort – despite rebuffs, the account manager will need to make multiple contacts with the prospect to keep her name in front of the prospect.

3. Multiple contacts – in order to be there at the right time, the account manager needs to:

   (a) contact the prospect six or more times a year;

   (b) use a combination of face-to-face, mail and phone contacts;

   (c) maintain contact activity for two or more years.

This approach takes time. To be consistent, it will require making the time to make multiple contacts… on schedule. Therefore, it is not an approach that you can afford to use on a large number of prospects. It is only for the best prospects – the top 20 per cent of prospects in a territory. It is reserved for those prospects who would be a significant addition to your portfolio and who, based on everything you know, meet your supplier criteria for asset quality, margins and relationship orientation.

Strategy no. 2: Educating the business owner

The objective of this strategy is to educate the prospect. It is possible through this strategy to help the business owner to see the relationship between his business objectives and his financing alternatives with greater clarity. And this increased clarity may result in a widening of the gap between the business owner's expectations and his current situation. An effective account manager is an educator – one who sees the business development process as an educational process. As an educator, he helps business owners think about several things:

1. Their current situation and probable future situations.

2. The problems that have been created by the current situation or may be created by a future situation.

3. The implications that those problems may have for the business or the business owner.

4. The need to change the current situation and to plan for future situations – and, most importantly, the payoff if the situation is improved or the consequence if it remains unchanged.

This education process starts the business owner thinking. This approach requires an account manager with excellent communication skills. The account manager must be able to talk about products and services, but more important, he must be able to get a good understanding of the business and the business owner. For example, the account manager needs to be comfortable discussing marketing approaches, production methods and processes, strategic plans and business and financial objectives, and he needs to understand where the business has been in the past, how the business got where it is today, and where it will be in three to five years.

By discussing these broader questions, the business owner begins to think out loud, and thinking out loud is the educational process. As he thinks through the points that were raised during the discussion, he is developing a better understanding of (1) the current situation and probable future situations, and (2) the problems and implications within each of these situations. If this kind of discussion were to take place multiple times, the business owner would begin to see any gaps more clearly and, when he perceived the gap to be large enough, he would feel compelled to take the necessary action to close it.

This business development strategy is an effective method of developing new business. However, to be successful, it requires two things:

- A series of substantive discussions with the business owner over a one- or two-year period. These discussions require careful planning, good research and excellent strategic selling skills.

- The willingness to keep at it even if the business owner isn't initially responsive.

Focusing on key prospects

Both of these strategies require consistent and persistent calling activity. In either case, the account manager will need to make multiple calls with enough frequency that an impact is made on the business owner. However, since all account managers have responsibilities in addition to business development and since these strategies require a commitment of persistence and consistency, these approaches can only be utilized for a relatively small number of prospects. In most cases, you will need to focus on a small number of carefully chosen prospects. These carefully selected prospects can be called *key prospects*. But how do you identify the prospects that are worth the time and effort required by these strategies? Generally, several steps are required.

First, look at your existing customer base and establish profiles for the types of customers that have helped your supplier meet its business objectives in the past. For example, you could build a list of your best customers and then carefully analyse their characteristics (sales size, location, products used, etc.). An analysis of these best customers will determine profiles for your existing key relationships. Second, will the types of businesses that have been most profitable for the supplier in the past continue to be the most profitable in the future? Now you'll need to assess the profiles from Step 1 for future growth and profitability. If the assessment is positive then these profiles become your profile businesses and any prospects that match the profiles are targeted as potential key prospects.

Third, project the profiles on to a database of businesses in your market areas. The results will be a list of key prospects: prospective clients that match your profiled businesses. Fourth, take a look at the business conditions in your market and determine industry segments that are growing. By comparing growing segments with your experience and understanding of those segments, you can identify any of those segments that are good target niches. Use databases to identify businesses within those segments that might be appropriate customers for your supplier. These identified businesses are now added to the list of key prospects.

The steps described above will generate two important lists for you, your sales managers and your account managers:

1. A list of key prospects that have a high probability of meeting the supplier's goals for asset quality, ROA and relationship orientation.

2. A list of your top 20 per cent of customers. (This list is generated in Step 1. Some suppliers use this list to shift the focus of

their relationship management effort. At this point, some sales managers request their account managers to develop a formal account plan for these relationships. The account plan focuses on both protecting the relationship – you can't afford to lose a top 20 per cent customer – and growing the relationship.)

Now, effort will need to be actively guided toward key customers and key prospects.

Some keys to success

The key to success in a focused business development effort is to keep your name or your ideas in front of the prospect often enough and over a long enough period of time to ensure that you are there when a need arises. Therefore, business development activity needs to be managed so that (1) it is directed toward the right clients and prospects, and (2) it continues over a long enough period of time to get results.

It sounds easy – but is it? A focused approach is difficult for account managers for several reasons:

- Proactively developing new clients is difficult, frustrating and often uncomfortable – and there is little immediate reward for the efforts expended.

- Most account managers have other responsibilities – existing business makes it difficult to find the time to make prospecting calls, develop referral sources, etc.

- Account managers get paid for putting business on the books this quarter or this year – not for thinking about next year's business.

- Many suppliers have a management focus on meeting goals for this quarter and this year, not next year or the year after – yet bringing in high-quality new businesses can take 12 months or more.

Given these issues, it's easy to see why 'shotgun' approaches to business development are easier for both a supplier and its account managers. Blitzes, promotional campaigns, telemarketing, direct mail, etc. can be done occasionally when you have the time or when things slow down. However, this creates a lack of consistency in the business development effort, since finding the time is dependent on many variables. As a result, these approaches are often inconsistent, hit or miss and ineffective – unless, of course, the economy is booming. A focused approach requires a consistent and persistent effort over a long period of time. It requires that the sales managers and the account managers make the time to be consistent and persistent. As a result, if a supplier chooses to use a focused approach, it will also need to develop a more active approach to sales management. It will require sales managers to actively direct and guide the business development activities of the account managers to ensure that there is a consistent and persistent effort on the part of every account manager. In effect, the sales manager will need to manage not only the short-term sales activity (meeting this month's goals), but also the long-term business development activity (today's prospects are next year's clients).

What is active sales management?

Many suppliers already have taken the first steps in sales management. They have established sales goals and call goals, defined territories and built some form of a prospect list. These are necessary steps, but they often result in passive sales management – where the account managers are responsible for providing their own direction and guidance, and consequently, their business develop-ment efforts are only as good as their individual experience.

The next step in sales management is a more active approach which provides a high degree of direction and ongoing guidance for both the sales management team and the account managers. To accomplish this, an additional set of sales management tools is required. For example:

- The development of a formal sales management hierarchy from the CEO down. This is not a separate sales management structure, but the explicit understanding that sales management is a part of every line manager's responsibilities. (Believe it or not, you don't need to have excellent selling skills to be an outstanding sales manager.)

- Each sales manager at each level of the organization is responsible for developing a formal sales plan for her level, and is accountable for the attainment of that sales plan.

- Each sales manager is accountable for developing and implementing formal business development strategies for achieving the plan for her area.

- Monthly sales meetings for all sales managers. These meetings provide a time and place for the sales management team to discuss their common concerns.

- A formal reporting system that tracks planned calls, client calls, prospecting calls, business booked and deals in the pipeline.

- The clear understanding that each account manager is fully responsible and accountable for her territory.

These additional tools begin to put active sales management systems in effect. But, in order to be successful, the sales managers also will have to shift the commercial business development culture of the supplier toward one that is more planned, proactive, organized and structured. This new focus will require sales managers to create an environment where there is:

- a strong sense of direction for account managers – an explicit definition of the businesses the supplier wants to go after and the overall strategy that will be used to bring them in;

- ongoing guidance for account managers – the sales managers and the account managers working together to develop overall and specific strategies that get results;

- a high level of coaching and counselling on business development skills;

- a high degree of visibility – everyone's business develop-ment activities are very visible to everyone else;

- a high degree of account planning for key accounts;

- a high level of preparation for calls on prospective customers.

This shift in focus and environment is really a change in culture: it requires a change in thinking and a change in sales behaviours, it requires new skills and new strategies, and it creates all the discomfort that goes along with change. In order to make these changes permanent, sales managers will need to help account managers become comfortable with these new skills and behaviours until they become the norm. It is the sales management team who will need to lead this change process.

Some suggestions for your calling programme

Successful calling programmes seem to have several characteristics in common. Some of these characteristics have been put in the form of suggestions and are listed below.

1. Be sure that you have formulated and articulated a clear and well-defined business development strategy that account managers can use to guide their activities.

2. Have each account manager develop a key account list and a key prospect list. These are formal lists and they need to be carefully reviewed with the sales manager.

3. Begin proactive calling now – don't wait until everything is perfect (the economy is good, your tracking system is in place, sales training is delivered, etc.). Discussing real-life experiences with peers and high-performers is the fastest way to become comfortable with a new set of skills and behaviours. And most

studies show that account managers learn more from real-life experience and coaching than they do from sales training.

4. Focus face-to-face calling on key relationships and key prospects, and use more indirect methods for non-key prospects. Carefully define what those indirect methods are.

5. Establish monthly sales meetings. A good sales meeting has an agenda, is highly structured, brings visibility to individual calling efforts, provides recognition and acknowledgment for high performers and continually develops sales skills. Administrative, operational and credit-related issues should not be discussed in a sales meeting.

6. Require call plans and call summaries. Proactive calling can be planned, so ask account managers to plan their calls a month in advance. Review the results of the calls at each sales meeting.

7. Provide regular strategy and skill coaching. This is the key to improving sales results. Don't try to coach on a joint call – it takes extensive coaching experience to stay objective on joint calls. Instead (1) review the call plan of each account manager, (2) select a key call, (3) contact the account manager and discuss the call before it is made.

8. Constantly refine the strategies and skills of the account managers by doing the following:

    (a) discussing new ways of thinking about business development, new client development, and the role of the account manager in a competitive environment;

(b) developing and refining the strategic selling skills that will help win clients in an increasingly competitive market.

(c) continually reinforcing the new strategies and skills until the new ways of thinking become culturally valued and a part of the job. (This is critical. Some account managers think that this focus won't last. We've seen these kinds of programmes before. They always go away. Ensure they are aware of the importance of these new skills and strategies.)

Taking your company into the international marketplace

The next section deals with points you need to consider before undertaking international expansion.

First things first

Why should I think about going international?
What size do I need to be to go international?
What are the key success factors for companies in my area entering the international market?
What should I expect from an international effort?
How much should I budget to launch an international effort?
How long should it take for an international effort to generate revenue?
Will I need extra staff to support an international effort?
Are there any specific issues that I need to be aware of?

Market issues

What are the ten largest international markets in my area of business?
What are the best international markets to go after?
How many markets should I go after?
How can I test an international market before I put a lot of effort into it?
Are there any international markets that I should avoid?
Are territories defined by country boundaries or are there regional definitions?

Channel issues

What are the different channel options available in going international?
When does it make sense to use international distributors?
When does it make sense to have a reseller channel?
When does it make sense to set up my own office(s) internationally?
Should I have a website?
If I develop a channel, can I still sell direct to companies that come to me through my website?
Is selling direct via the web a good option?
What are some of the barriers to selling from my website?

Product translation and localization

Does our product need to be translated and localized before it goes international?

What is the difference between translation and localization?
What if I just want to translate the product? What is involved?
What are the different ways to handle the translation?
What else is involved if I want to localize my product?
Should I have an international reseller handle my product translation or should I manage the process myself?
Do I have to translate and reprint all of my marketing materials for every country?

Intellectual property protection

What is a trademark?
How are trademarks established?
How and why do trademark disputes arise?
What is involved in registering a trademark?
What is the difference between TM (trademark), SM (service mark) and ® (registration symbol)?
What countries provide the best anti-piracy protection?
What countries provide the least anti-piracy protection?

Pricing, credit and payment issues

What are the best ways to get paid for international orders?
Should I grant credit terms to my resellers?
Should I charge the reseller an up-front fee for becoming a reseller?
What discount level will I have to offer to international resellers?
How are maintenance fees usually handled outside my country?
Should pricing be in my currency or the local currency?

Will I have to worry about withholding taxes and, if so, how do they work?

What do we have to take into consideration in relation to ordering, shipping and returns?

Setting up a subsidiary

What are the advantages of setting up a company-owned subsidiary?
What are the disadvantages?
Is there a point at which it makes sense to set up a subsidiary?
How much should I budget for a small office?
What else should I consider before deciding to set up a subsidiary?
If I want to set up a main office in another country, are some countries better than others?
Do some countries offer investment incentives?

Recruiting a channel

Where can I find good prospects?
What should I do when an international reseller contacts me asking to represent my product in their country?
How do we handle resellers that demand market exclusivity?
How do we handle cross-border sales, where a reseller in one market sells to a multinational company with offices in other markets where we have a reseller?
How can I protect myself so I don't get locked out of a territory by someone who is underperforming?
How do I determine if a territory has too many or too few reseller partners?

Are there countries where I can have multiple resellers?

How do I qualify resellers to ensure that they are reputable organizations and will generate sales?

Is there an ideal size of reseller organization?

Should I use a reseller application and, if so, what are the key elements?

What are some key indicators that a prospective international company will be a good partner to do business with?

Legal issues

Do I really need a comprehensive international reseller agreement?

What is a reasonable term for an agreement?

Are exclusivity clauses enforceable?

Should I require a non-compete clause?

What are the most common reasons for terminating a contract?

If I want to terminate, how do I notify the reseller so that I am protected under the contract?

What happens upon termination?

What should we use as governing law, that of my country or the foreign country?

Will foreign resellers be able to read and understand my contract? Is there a better way to start the relationship?

Marketing issues

What are some ways to help international resellers keep focus on selling my product(s)?

What should I require in a monthly report?

What type of marketing materials will I need to supply resellers?

How do I go about finding information on local marketing resources such as mailing lists and local publications?

Support

What type of tools and documentation do I need to best help facilitate an ongoing relationship with an international partner?

Will the reseller need any training?

What types of training do I need to provide?

How do I go about providing training to international partners in various countries?

What is the best way to handle ongoing communications with international partners?

Should I schedule visits to our resellers?

What are the most common marketing support and incentive programmes?

Should I have reseller conferences, and if so, what is involved?

What if things don't work out? Is it easy to terminate a reseller?

How do I best leverage existing support infrastructure and resources to support international partners?

What is considered to be an acceptable level of response time for product support questions?

What level of technical support should I expect an international partner to provide to their market?

What is generally considered to be acceptable terms and conditions relative to warranties and maintenance?

I am thinking of hiring an international manager. What type of person should I be looking for?

What would their responsibilities be within my organization?

Where can I find people with this profile and background?

CHAPTER 9

Product realization

Costs involved in the design process

The primary coordinates of value are quality and cost. Market timing is also important, but can be viewed as the dynamic nature of quality. Quality is defined by customer desires. Quality function deployment (QFD) is a process by which one can deploy quality into the product; into the system to bring forth, sustain and retire the product; and into the enterprise as a whole. Within QFD, we deploy quality to ensure that the customer gets what he wants. But what about cost?

From the perspective of an individual, cost is a measure of value in that a consumer is willing to trade money for value. From the perspective of a project, a project is driven by value, which is potential energy. As time proceeds, the cost of a project grows and the residual value to be realized decreases. If too much cost is incurred relative to the initial value of the project, measured in terms of what the customer is willing to spend, then the residual value at the end of the project is negative. Simply put, cost deployment is a means of designing for cost.

Cost deployment

The basic concept underlying cost deployment to date is to match value with cost. Suppose that we have a system with known parts. If we can determine the importance of these parts by some evaluation process and the cost of those parts, we can then divide the importance of each part by the total importance to obtain the relative importance for each part. We can also divide the cost of each part by the total cost to obtain the relative cost of each part.

Cost databases and quality function deployment

When the cost database is coupled with quality function deployment, a very important database emerges. It contains an instance of combined quality and cost data. The evaluation of alternatives for the cost reduction of the selected parts provides additional instances. Multiple instances permit the application of statistical processes to determine equations that can predict cost in terms of quality characteristics. This offers the potential for quality-based cost estimating. With this database we can apply cost analysis toward that target.

Cost deployment

Cost deployment assumes that the product has been decomposed into mechanisms and parts that perform given product functions. The sum of the costs of the mechanisms that provide the function, along with the cost of integrating them, is the cost of the product function. Not all product quality characteristics will be statistically significant. In addition, some objects may have no statistically significant quality characteristics. For these reasons, cost deployment should proceed cautiously. Direct estimation of the cost at the mechanism or function level may turn out to be more accurate than at the part level. Hence, in moving toward cost deployment, one should start at the highest possible level to test the viability in terms of the specific product or product line.

Personal estimating experience indicates that approximately 80 per cent of the advantage of reducing cost lies within the process to bring forth the product. The remaining 20 per cent has to do with product quality characteristics. To get the full effect of cost drivers, cost deployment must include quality characteristics of the system to bring forth the product, as well as the quality characteristics of the product. Both discrete and continuous quality characteristics may be needed to describe this problem.

Current processes and their capabilities

From my experience of visiting companies, touring their manufacturing or distribution processes, and talking with their staff about where they are today, one thing seems quite consistent. These processes usually perform exceptionally well in producing quality products that meet technical requirements. However, these processes were usually not designed to minimize costs or the cycle time from order entry to shipment. Some of the characteristics of these processes include:

- The product is routed around the plant to various work centres where work is staged and waits to be processed.

- WIP (work in progress) inventory is typically four to eight weeks.

- Raw material inventory typically turns less than 10 times per year. Inventory consists of too much of what is not needed, and too little of what is needed.

- Indirect labour is needed to locate and expedite orders, which also affects the schedule of orders currently in the process.

- Customers are demanding increasingly shorter delivery schedules. Product is picked from the plant room, processed and put back into the plantroom awaiting the next pick.

- You may not be able to see the progression of product build on the shop floor.

The result of all this is increased cycle time, increased labour costs, increased inventory and missed deliveries. Management time is spent handling customer complaints rather than implementing a competitive strategy.

The market needs

The customer demands on-time delivery and, in the case of spare parts, wants unplanned needs to be met overnight. He wants low costs yet will pay a premium for consistent on-time delivery. In short, the customer wants lean, responsive suppliers dedicated to fulfilling his need – flexibility. These market demands can be consistently met with improved processes.

The benefits of cellular manufacturing

Manufacturing cells get their name because the people, processes and equipment are organized into areas or spaces called cells. The key difference between this manufacturing approach and that described above is the product stays within this area rather than being moved around the plant and staged for various operations such as machining, welding, assembly and testing.

These cells are typically arranged into a U shape, which conserves space, promotes a team environment within the cell and simplifies incoming and finished goods logistics. Because all the resources (people and processes) are available within the cell, there is no competition for those resources and therefore products move rapidly through the cell. Labour resources are focused on producing the end item rather than maximizing the efficiency of one particular operation. The result is a better flow of the finished product to the customer and more cash available to the company.

The expected benefits from cellular manufacturing include:

- Cycle times of days rather than weeks, typically a 70 per cent reduction.

- Shipments weekly or daily rather than at the end of the month.

- Dramatic reductions in inventory, typically 50 per cent.

- Opportunity to bill customers daily rather than monthly.

- Dramatic reductions in indirect labour, typically 50 per cent.

- Less direct labour for the build, typically 10 per cent.

- An increase in capacity, typically 50 per cent.

- A more profitable business, typically 25 per cent more net income.

The design process

Several elements of cell design are very important. First, the process steps must be described and allocated to the employees and processes within the cell. It is very important to equally load (balance) each employee with work. This means that if worker 1 spends 20 minutes performing the operation at the first position then worker 2 should spend 20 minutes performing the operations at the second position and so on. Now this will never be perfectly achievable, but it can usually be achieved within practical limitations. Because of the variability in processing from piece to piece and person to person, I always plan for a small buffer between operations, typically only one piece. This increases the labour utilization, increases shipments, and provides limited flexibility to employees for short breaks and training assistance from fellow employees.

It is important to establish a team atmosphere and for management to support frequent team meetings. This team becomes the continuous improvement mechanism for the manufacturing cells. In situations where there are multiple teams competition often develops between the cells for output and quality. For example, if a designer needs to choose between several production sources by comparing costs and delivery times, he needs to know the relationships between possible tolerances he might specify and the cost and time capabilities of various methods or suppliers. If a supplier is to provide a fixture for joining three parts, he needs to have geometric models of the parts indicating where they will join, how the main dimensional requirements of the final assembly are linked through the various parts, and where the fixture is permitted to attach to them. If a final assembler finds that the parts do not fit, he needs to be able to trace back, through the web, the various parts, dimensions, tolerances, fixtures and their suppliers in order to find the root cause and design an effective solution.

To accomplish the move from reactive to proactive, and to capture information in ways that support proactive transactions, we need tools that identify clusters of transactions, methods of visualizing and managing the web, systematic ways of defining information that is passed out on to the web, and methods of maintaining control over the coherence of that information until the dispersed processes and their outputs converge again as the product is made and assembled.

Analysing your business for synchronous manufacturing

Being synchronous means being proficient at change. This allows an organization to do anything it wants to do whenever it wants to. Thus a synchronous organization can employ business process re-engineering (BPR) as a core competency when transformation is called for. It can hasten its conversion to lean production while that is still useful. And, importantly, it can continue to succeed when constant innovation becomes the dominant competitive strategy. Holding off synchronous programmes until a transformation to lean production is completed wrongly assumes that these are sequentially dependent concepts. Rather than close the stable door after the horse has bolted, a transformation to lean production will happen faster and with less expense as the organization becomes more synchronous.

Decreasing innovation cycles in all market sectors are increasing the frequency of new product introduction. The process of bringing new or improved products to market involves changes in the production area. Whether these changes are small or sweeping, there is usually a transition period of adjustment and settling in. During this transition period, two principal sources of turmoil are at work: (1) as changed items are put to the test of use, some fine-tuning may be required before they satisfy their purpose, and (2) the interaction of the changed item with its environment may have some undesirable side-effects that need to be resolved.

A new machine or production cell introduced into the production environment requires a shakeout of the machine itself, integration of the machine into its interactive environment, operator training, maintenance training and service training, to name the easy parts. Then we have the operational idiosyncrasies and failure modes that are learned the hard way by experience.

An obvious way to reduce the toll of transition is to reduce the quantity of things in transition. If we want to do this while accommodating more new products than ever before, we have to learn how to build new products with old proven process-reusable processes, configurable for a new purpose. Reusability and configuration are construction concepts – they have to do with the way things are built, no matter whether these things are manufacturing cells, work procedures, production teams or information automation systems. To bring a new or improved product to market, we want to introduce as little new process as possible. For instance, instead of designing and building a completely new welding cell we might duplicate and modify an existing well-understood cell. This cell will have some new elements in it to accommodate the variations of the new product, but most of the cell will be familiar. It may not be as technically appealing as a completely new design, but it will be up and running a lot faster, more cheaply, with less scrap and rework and more predictability.

This does not mean an end to capital investment or a continuous cannibalism of used equipment. It means an important new focus on the structure of configurable production elements. And it is physical configuration we need, not programme configuration. We need the ability to make unanticipated new things from reusable pieces, not simply select some predefined subset of flexible capability or embedded options. Configurable structures, whether they organize sub-units in a piece of equipment, equipment relationships in a cell, cell relationships in a production area or production areas in a plant, require some form of module reusability.

For maximum change proficiency these structures must be scalable as well as reusable and configurable. Scalability eliminates size restrictions imposed by the structure, allowing any number of reusable modules to be included or omitted as desired. The synchronous enterprise has been defined as one that is proficient at change. This usually means that it is agile, and agility is very important in change proficiency. Competency is an umbrella word that we often use to encompass qualities that are hard to quantify. Nevertheless, a practical measure of agility is needed before we can talk meaningfully about getting more of it, or even getting some of it.

You can change virtually anything if cost is no object. However, if your cost of change is too high relative to your competitor's costs, there will be a steady erosion of working capital, or at least a higher tax on shareholder profits. Change at any cost is not viable. If it was, we need not restructure anything ever – we can simply throw out the old and buy a new capability, assuming, of course, that we can bring something new to the operational level quick enough.

To measure proficiency at change we need quantified statements for each of the four proficiency metrics. Ideally, in order to analyse existing situations, we want to find quantities that are already in our books, or that can be constructed from historical records. The time of a change can be likened to the time-to-market of a new product. In this case, we are talking about the change activity associated with creating a new cash-generating customer transaction. Time-to-market is that time associated with product and process design and implementation that results in a deliverable cash transaction with a customer, and includes the formation and management of effective customer and supplier relationships. Similarly, cost-to-market of a change is the cost required for completion – or in our new product example, that first cash transaction.

Continuing with our new product metaphor, though new products may be rolling off the line, we know that neither the product nor the process design is solid in the early days of delivery. There may be some rework and scrap beyond our desired levels. During this early period we often have a functionality shortfall from our targets, and generally have a difficulty in quality-level predictability.

Robustness measures the strength and competency (quality) of our change process. It can be measured in the same ways that we measure the quality of anything: by customer satisfaction polls, by degree/amount of shortfall, etc. Robustness is a statement about our ability to predict the satisfactory completion of a change activity. How often have we been on time, on budget, on specification (or at least within acceptable variances of our original predictions)? If we are generally correct then we probably have a high robustness to our change process.

Lost opportunities are those occasions when a change could have provided some useful advantage but was declined. Opportunities are presented to producers by prospective customers. An opportunity must fit within the producer's vision and mission to qualify as an opportunity. An innovation is a self-initiated change on the part of a producer, and is presented to the customer. It might be in the form of a new product, a lower-cost product, a higher-quality product or a faster product. Some innovations are bigger than others – a 20 per cent cost reduction is twice as big as a 10 per cent cost reduction. The customer provides the innovation points according to how innovative they feel they are. There is no incentive to leak out three successive innovations that are equivalent to one leaping innovation which encompasses all three if somewhere in the succession a competitor establishes a new benchmark. Catching up is not innovation.

Meeting variations in production demand is another major issue today, whether we are talking about short-term surge capacity or the ability to track longer-term market demand changes. In the car industry, for example, a high fixed break-even point for a car plant is an example of a downside barrier to capacity change, and the inability of one plant to make another plant's product is an upside barrier.

Business re-engineering is another high-profile change activity with poor general proficiency. Recent studies indicate that only about 20 per cent of these activities achieve their desired ends, even though billions of dollars are involved on a national scale. Generally a company that is unsuccessful with a re-engineering project will try again and again until it gets it right. Studies explain that this is part of the learning process; however, the principal lesson seems to be that you can't stop until you're finished, whereas a better lesson is the knowledge that you are never finished. Unfortunately, companies feel successful when they have migrated from an old mode of operation to a new entrenched position.

Organizational learning is another vital, but elusive, capability today. It is the mechanism that develops new core competency. The knowledge base that is the substance of core competency is vulnerable to both personnel loss and rapid obsolescence. Captured and constantly renewed, an effective knowledge base will steadily migrate the organization's core competencies in sync with changing technologies.

Production changeover is a current issue in most industries. Major car companies are moving from an 8–12 week plant shutdown for retooling to a targeted 1–3 week cycle over the next few years, driven by competitors who are already there. Semiconductor manufacturers with a higher frequency of new model introductions are trying to squeeze small prototype runs through their production facilities with minimal disruption to the revenue stream. Defence manufacturers often win or lose contracts on the basis of changeover costs and times. In its best form, changeover is a reconfiguration issue, taking existing resources and configuring them differently for a different purpose.

Creating a contract that defines and fosters a functioning business relationship is a hot issue today. Contract procedures and negotiations that outlive opportunity windows, inhibit opportunity consideration or consume resources without value have been recognized as pernicious for some time now. The process of creating a new product is receiving a lot of attention in most industries. Concurrent engineering has given way to product realization, which encompasses the entire concept-to-cash process. This area gains in importance as the competitive focus moves from cost to innovation.

High variety, small-lot manufacturing and mass customization are issues popularly associated with agility. Both are examples of real-time change-proficiency during the performance of production operations. Expedited production orders are another example of change during the performance of the production operation. Though all are major issues in defence industries where small quantity and job-shop practices prevail, mass producers are valuing the advantages of proficiency in the performance–time change area as well.

Continuous improvement seems at first to belong to other paradigms than agility; however, the principles of synchronous systems enable and facilitate continuous improvement rather than simply mandating it. Software is playing an increasing role in the operation of our factories and the infrastructure of companies – yet making a simple upgrade or improvement is postponed as long as possible, since unpredictable disruption to service is inevitable.

Hidden in every sizable company is a wealth of innovative techniques that will improve its competitiveness – if they are recognized and diffused to the rest of the organization. How do you find the pearls? How do you get the rest of the organization interested in something they didn't invent?

Mobilizing embedded corporate knowledge is a cornerstone of synchronous competition. If a company is going to accelerate its proactive and reactive capabilities, it cannot afford to reinvent the same solutions over and over again, it cannot afford to make the same mistakes over and over again, it cannot afford large changes when small ones will do, and it cannot afford to ignore the pearls that go begging for recognition.

Leverage comes from reusable knowledge, configurable for different applications across the entire corporation. The principal asset in corporations today is collective knowledge – something that doesn't show on the balance sheet. The value of that asset is multiplied by its mobility within the corporation. Most companies today have not thought about that knowledge base, how it changes and how it is deployed at points that need it while it still has something to offer.

The list below discusses important factors in organizational change.

- *Organizational structure.* Discuss the organization relative to its structure. How are responsibilities compartmentalized? What are the organizational units and sub-units? What are the standard mechanisms and events of inter-unit interaction? How are decisions and approvals obtained? What is organizationally rigid and what is fluid? Are teaming concepts employed? What about cross-functional teams? When was the last reorganization and what was its nature?

- *Human resources.* Discuss the human factors for all employees. What forms of training and education exist? Is cross-functional training available? To what degree are people empowered? How are hiring and downsizing accomplished? What mobility exists within the plant, within the corporation and within the community for employees? Are unique, difficult or rare skill sets involved? When an open or new position is filled, is there a ripple effect among other employee positions? What is the general access-to-information situation? What surprise events have occurred in this area in the last 24 months that have required a response.

- *Operating procedures.* Discuss standardized policy and operating procedures. Is there a standard procedure for new product start-ups or for factory conversion? What operating procedures apply to the production activity? What requires approval signatures and how long do they take? What events have caused procedures to be implemented and/or modified? What performance metrics are used within the plant and by whom? Discuss work rules and speed of responsiveness to unexpected production needs.

- *Information automation.* Discuss the management information services (MIS) and decision support computer-related environment. What kind of operating and management reports are available? What kind of general information is accessible? To what degree are personnel supported with desktop access? How often have these been updated and modified? What kind of shopfloor reporting exists? What role does simulation and modelling play? What project management tools are used? Describe an event where a change to the system was desired but did not (or could not) occur. What forms of electronic communication exist – and between whom? How are engineering changes dealt with? Are suppliers and customers tied electronically to the plant in any way?

- *Control automation.* Discuss the automation control environment. What systems, hardware and software are in use? Discuss a case where an improvement was implemented. Discuss the backlog of unimplemented improvements and corrections. How is control code developed and maintained? How do new controls enter the plant? How are controls and their systems maintained? How is training for new technology accomplished?

- *Facility.* Discuss the physical plant facility relative to its fixed and flexible nature. Has the plant ever been configured? What restrictions exist in adding equipment and processing capabilities? Discuss the utilities (electric, gas, steam, sewage, toxic disposal, etc.) required by the production process, and their fixed and flexible natures. Discuss the procedures involved in relocating or obtaining new utility service in the physical plant. How is equipment relocated, installed and removed?

- *Material movement/management.* Discuss material, WIP and finished goods movement and storage within the facility. Discuss JIT implementation and examples of when it fails – such as material not available when needed from both internal and external sources.

- *Production process.* Discuss production process issues. What is the capacity utilization of the processes in place? Do capacity require-ments fluctuate? How is the plant scheduled? How does installed process technology compare to the state of the art? What changes in process technology are taking place and what does the future require? When was the process last changed, why and with what procedure? Are workstations or work areas ever idle because of upstream or downstream stoppages? What forms of flexibility exist in the process? What is the human role in the process? What kind of process characterization knowledge exists? What is the role, if any, of simulation and modelling?

- *Production equipment.* Discuss the general state of production equipment. What degree of automation exists? What degree of flexibility exists? What range of materials can be accommodated? What unique single-point equipment has caused the biggest problem when it is down? How does installed equipment compare to the state-of-the-art? What is the turnover and upgrade of equipment technology? What does the future require that is not currently present? Are unique and/or rare skills required for any equipment? What is the nature and state of operator and maintenance training? What are equipment utilization and failure rates? Where would you like to make a change but can't? What kind of process characterization knowledge exists? What is the role, if any, of simulation and modelling? What degree of variation and commonality exists among equipment types?

- *Changeover/setup system.* Discuss the changeover and setup processes. How often do they occur? What are the procedures? How is equipment utilization affected? What are the cycle times? How is a new product introduced to the production environment – and how frequently does this occur?

- *Supply chain.* Discuss the supply chain and supporting logistics. How stable is the supply chain? What is the procedure for gaining new suppliers? What is supplier turnover? Describe an unexpected supplier failure that was costly. How flexible are supplier contracts? What is the JIT situation and performance history?

- *Distribution chain.* Discuss the customer interface and logistical support. How is business obtained? How is the customer interface conducted? How are product orders obtained and received? How often are product orders modified – and with what lead time? What are the trends in this area? What are the sizes and frequencies of orders? How many product types are there? What shipping alternatives exist? What finished-goods inventory exists? What are customer delivery-time expectations and trends?

Product realization

The fundamental objective in product realization is to turn ideas into something of value in the marketplace.

The ability to clearly and logically communicate ideas, information and data orally and in written form to others in a way that maximizes ease of manufacture by simplifying the design through part capability, developing modular designs, minimizing part variation, designing a part to be multifunctional or meeting customer demands is vital. Top management should ensure the effective and efficient operation of realization and support processes and the associated process network, so that the organization has the capability of satisfying its interested parties. While realization processes result in products that add value to the organization, support processes are also necessary to the organization and add value indirectly. Appendix A contains a product realization checklist for your organization.

CHAPTER 10

Lean business system self-assessment

The purpose of self-assessment

This self-assessment is provided as a tool for suppliers to evaluate their progress toward implementing a lean business system. The four categories (organizational environment, systems, tools and techniques, and metrics) form the foundation for a holistic approach to a lean business system – an approach that engages the entire organization in the drive to eliminate waste.

This assessment is for organizations to assess their progress toward implementing a lean business system and to uncover areas where focused activities need to occur to spur improvement.

Using the self-assessment questionnaire

1. Select a representative sample of the organization (comprising all levels and all functions) to fill out the assessment. A sample size of 2 per cent to 10 per cent based on organization size would be appropriate.

2. Gather the completed assessments and compile the results.

3. Results can then be analysed and used as part of the management review, strategic planning and goal-setting activity, or shared with the organization at large.

Directions

Answer each statement or question in the following categories by putting a score in the right-hand column that best indicates your assessment of that activity. The scale is from 1 to 7, broken down as follows:

1 = No implementation of the item: it hasn't been addressed by the organization.

2 = To a very little extent: very little awareness of the item in the organization.

3 = To some extent: the item is in the early stages of being addressed.

4 = To a moderate extent: the item is in the middle of being addressed.

5 = To a large extent: the item has been addressed and data on results is available.

6 = To a great extent: the item is fully implemented and complete results are available.

7 = To a superior extent: results for the item indicate world-class or industry benchmark.

Category 1: Organizational environment

Sub-category A: Top management support

To what extent have top management (including CEO, president, vice-president(s), general managers, directors, etc.) shown support for lean business systems by doing the following:

Item	Score
1. Visibly promoting lean business systems in words and action?	
2. Committing time to planning for lean business system activities and reviewing progress?	
3. Holding their managers and supervisors accountable for implementing lean business system activities?	
4. Making implementation of and involvement in lean business systems a part of the formal review process for managers and supervisors?	
5. Recognizing managers' and employees' lean business systems initiatives and continuous improvement innovations?	
6. Investing resources (including capital and time) in identifying and implementing lean business system initiatives?	
7. Encouraging or mandating employees at all levels to be involved and participate in lean business systems initiatives?	

Sub-category B: Employee involvement

To what extent has there been involvement of employees through the following:

Item	Score
1. Cross-functional teams for problem solving and continuous improvement?	
2. Participation by bargaining unit representatives in planning and review activities for lean business system initiatives?	
3. The establishment of a cross-functional steering group or review body for the lean business system approach?	

Sub-category C: Organizational buy-in and support

To what extent has the concept of lean business systems been embraced and supported by:

Item	Score
1. The employee population in general?	
2. The bargaining unit hierarchy?	
3. The manufacturing organization?	
4. The engineering organization?	
5. The maintenance organization?	
6. The production planning and scheduling organization?	
7. The purchasing organization?	
8. The management support organization (including accounting, human resources (HR), etc.)?	

Sub-category D: Organizational alignment

How effectively has the organization dealt with:

Item	Score
1. Employee concerns for job security relating to the elimination of waste?	
2. Employee concerns about rewards for lean business systems involvement?	
3. Establishing a philosophy or policy statement that articulates what the organization is trying to accomplish with the lean business systems approach?	
4. Promoting an environment of continuous improvement with a never-ending quest for waste elimination?	
5. Promoted continuous learning and skill building at all levels of the organization?	

Category 2: Systems

Sub-category A: Production systems

To what extent have the following systems been implemented?

Item	Score
1. A pull system for customer orders.	
2. A material handling system for material flow through production.	
3. A manufacturing control system (including visual controls).	
4. A JIT system for work in process.	
5. A JIT system for external suppliers.	

6. A Kaizen (lean manufacturing) system for continuous improvement.
7. A cell manufacturing system to create one-piece flow.

Sub-category B: Maintenance systems

To what extent have the following systems been implemented?

Item	Score
1. A maintenance schedule for all production machinery.	
2. A system for managing unscheduled maintenance/breakdown repair.	
3. A system for evaluating maintenance performance and adjusting preventive maintenance activities.	

Sub-category C: Scheduling systems

To what extent have the following systems been implemented?

Item	Score
1. A system for level and balanced schedules for production.	
2. A system for evaluating schedule performance and adjusting production schedules.	

Sub-category D: Supplier management systems

To what extent have the following systems been implemented?

Item	Score
1. A system for supplier involvement and development.	
2. A strategy that translates the organization's business plan into supply base requirements.	
3. A system for establishing gain-sharing relationships with key suppliers.	
4. A system for identifying key suppliers and rationalizing the supplier base.	
5. A system for accurately and fairly measuring subcontractor performance.	
6. A system for supply chain management that fully satisfies the requirements.	
7. A system for subcontractor quality system development with the goal of subcontractor compliance.	
8. A system for assuring subcontractor investment in lean systems and continuous improvement.	

Sub-category E: Product planning and development systems

To what extent have the following systems been implemented?

Item	Score
1. A system for supplier involvement in design and product planning activities.	
2. A system for soliciting and reacting to supplier input for product changes and enhancements.	
3. A system for cross-functional involvement in design and product planning activities.	
4. A system for soliciting and reacting to operational input for product changes and enhancements.	
5. A mechanism for customer involvement in design and product planning activities.	

Sub-category F: Information systems

To what extent have the following systems been implemented?

Item	Score
1. A cohesive system for electronic communication and data sharing with customers.	
2. A cohesive system for electronic communication and data sharing with suppliers.	
3. A shop floor data collection and dissemination system that supports material flow and the JIT system.	
4. A management information system that supports performance analysis and management decision making.	
5. A system that supports relevant quality planning requirements.	

Category 3: Tools and techniques

Sub-category A: Lean manufacturing tools

To what extent have the following tools and techniques been implemented?

Item	Score
1. Just-in-time (JIT).	
2. Cycle time reduction.	
3. Synchronous flow manufacturing.	
4. Manufacturing cells.	
5. Kanban system for product flow.	
6. Visual systems (including industrial housekeeping).	
7. Quick job changeover.	

8. Process control (including set-up sheets, control plans, job instructions and standardized work).
9. Value stream mapping.
10. Manufacturing simulation/process optimization.

Sub-category B: Problem solving and continuous improvement

To what extent have the following tools and techniques been implemented?

Item	Score
1. Kaizen/continuous improvement workshops.	
2. Process improvement/process mapping.	
3. Seven basic problem-solving tools (i.e. brainstorming, cause and effect diagrams, Pareto diagrams, histograms, graphs, checksheets, nominal group technique).	
4. Statistical process control (SPC).	
5. Benchmarking of best practices.	
6. Taguchi methods/design of experiments (DOE).	
7. Suggestion systems.	
8. Quality circles/continuous improvement teams/work group teams.	

Category 4: Metrics

Sub-category A: External performance metrics

To what extent are the following performance metrics being collected?

Item	Score
1. Parts per million defective.	
2. On-time delivery.	
3. Customer returns (non-product related).	
4. Missed customer requirements (not resulting in a customer return due to granting of an exemption or waiver; rework; regraded for alternate application; rejected or scrapped).	
5. Customer satisfaction ratings.	

Sub-category B: Internal performance metrics

To what extent are the following performance metrics being collected?

Item	Score
1. Work-in-process (WIP).	
2. Inventory turns.	
3. Days supply of finished product.	
4. Design to manufacture (product development cycle).	
5. Order cycle time (from receipt to shipment).	
6. Manufacturing cycle time (from release to finished product).	
7. Total downtime (as a percentage of total available hours to produce).	
8. Cost of quality (including detection, prevention and internal failure).	
9. Employee productivity (parts/pieces per person hour).	
10. Internal parts per million defective.	
11. Order processing time (from receipt to release).	

12. Product wait time (from finished product to shipment).
13. Shipment lead time (from dock to dock).

Sub-category C: How the metrics are used

To what extent are the following metrics used for improvement?

Item	Score
1. By upper management to set improvement targets.	
2. By middle management/supervisors to focus resources and activities for departmental improvement.	
3. By the workforce to gauge their performance and suggest areas for improvement.	
4. As feedstock to problem solving/continuous improvement teams for setting baselines and determining the scope of their issue.	
5. As a communication tool for the organization to show progress on continuous improvement.	

Lean business system self-assessment: results analysis

The results of processing

Once the completed assessments have been collected you should tabulate the results. The average score, the mean and the number of respondents should be calculated for each question, and an average for each of the four categories should be calculated as well.

Interpreting and using the results

There are several ways to use the results of this self-assessment. Whichever way you choose, bear in mind that the purpose of the assessment is to provide feedback to the management team on how well the implementation of lean business is going in your organization and to highlight areas of concern or lack of progress.

Individual item analysis

One way to use the results is to look at the average score for individual items.

Below 4 indicates an item the management team should investigate further. It may be that the item is not pertinent to your situation; if it is pertinent, it is not getting the attention it should. The team should use a problem-solving methodology to get to the root of the issue and develop an action plan to enhance the implementation of that item.

Between 4 and 6 indicates an item that is being implemented and some data on its effectiveness is available. The available data guides your decision making. If the data is good you may simply need to stay on that course and allow the item to be completely implemented. If the data is not satisfactory, then once again the management team should use a problem-solving process to determine which parts of the implementation of that item are unsatisfactory and develop an action plan to enhance them.

Above 6 indicates an item that is fully implemented and contributing fully to a lean business system. Items in this range can be used by the management team as a good example or a template for implementing other items in the organization. The quicker the learning from the successful implementation of one of the items can be spread through the organization, the more momentum your lean business system implementation will have.

Category analysis

Another way to interpret the results is by looking at the aggregate average within each of the four categories. By looking at each category, the management team may find that the overall implementation is strong in one category and weak in others. Once again the same scoring breakdown applies: below 4: investigate further; 4–6: stay the course; 6 or above: multiply the success. It should also be noted that if all categories are in the 4–6 range, the management team will get the most 'bang for their buck' by developing plans to enhance the organization's environment and systems categories.

Cautions and recommendations

This tool should only be used periodically. A good time would be after the first year of your lean business system implementation; early on, your aim should be to get results and make things happen. Where this tool can be particularly helpful is in prioritizing how to roll out the lean business system implementation. It is extremely important that you do not try to do the entire organization at once; this tool will help you establish priorities.

This tool, like many other assessment tools, should be used to spur improvement, not as a hammer to punish people with or to point out individual deficiencies. If it is used for anything but an improvement tool, its value to the organization will be compromised, and you will get less truthfulness and honesty in the responses. Also, if you violate the anonymity of the respondents, the same lack of honesty will show up in the results.

Integrating manufacturing planning and control systems into the supply chain

Manufacturing planning and control (MPC) systems play a vital internal role in manufacturing organizations, helping to develop overall and detailed material and capacity plans and schedules. When elements of a manufacturing organization's planning and scheduling are made known to supply chain partners, the linked companies can improve their respective supply chain performances.

Consider an organization XYZ that has limited information links with members of its supply chain. For downstream customers, XYZ must estimate (forecast) future demands. Most of the forecasting will be based on historical data, with some qualitative adjustments made for anticipated cultural and economic environmental changes. Orders will be placed, but the timing and quantities of the orders will vary from the forecast. XYZ's customers will also lack information about stock on hand that would be useful in preparing orders. For upstream suppliers, the same uncertainty will exist. Even if XYZ employs sophisticated internal planning and control systems, the risks of demand and supply uncertainties will affect operations and results. We will begin by describing manufacturing planning and control (MPC) systems.

Manufacturing planning and control systems

MPC has been defined as a system that provides information to efficiently manage the flow of materials, effectively utilize people and equipment, coordinate internal activities with those of suppliers, and communicate with customers about market requirements. The MPC system undertakes several activities to fulfil the information requirements of this definition. These activities are linked internally through various departments and hierarchies.

Within the front end, demand management includes activities to determine external (customer) demands and internal demands: forecasting, order entry, order promising, determining branch warehouse requirements, interplant orders and service parts requirements. Forecasting supports planning at all planning levels – long-, mid- and short-term. Within the short-term planning horizon, orders entered into the system constitute the forecast. Basically, until a definite order is placed by a customer or a firm requirement is made known for an internal need, all demands are estimated. Demand management is combined with resource planning to create aggregate production plans, and that planning data is reorganized to create the master production schedule (MPS).

The MPS then drives materials requirement planning (MRP) and capacity requirements planning (CRP) by exploding demand requirements through product specifications, like bills of materials (BOM) and routing files. Material needs are determined by netting the gross requirements for an item against inventory records containing on-hand balances and scheduled receipts. In time-phased planning, net requirements are used to determine when an order needs to be received and, based on lead time data, when it needs to be released to the shop floor or to a supplier. The material plans are sent to capacity requirements planning (CRP) to determine how much and when capacity is needed to carry out required manufacturing activities.

The outputs of MRP and CRP planning are schedules that are executed (in the back end) by sending orders to the shop floor (to make) and to suppliers (to buy). Fulfilment of orders by suppliers depends on their ability to meet the requirements of the order such as quantity, quality and due date.

External inputs to/outputs from the MPC system

The supply chain concept links an organization's domain with suppliers (upstream) and customers (downstream). What internal MPC information can the organization share with these linked units to improve supply chain performance? Assuming the keystone premises of supply chain relationships – information, communication, cooperation and trust – are met, knowledge about planned orders and inventory status can be as valuable externally as it is internally.

Two-way information sharing is valuable between the buying organization and the supplying organization. One useful information exchange would be for the customer to share planned order release information from its requirements planning system with the supplier. Typically, the supplier will forecast demands to prepare for future orders from the customer. In a make-to-stock environment, finished goods are scheduled to meet that forecast. These goods are then consumed by orders. In an assemble-to-order environment, modules are stocked so that orders can quickly be filled through execution of the final assembly schedule. And in a make-to-order environment, common components are ordered/built to reduce the cumulative lead time from order placement to shipment of the order. In all cases, having knowledge about the quantities and timing of customer requirements – in advance of receiving the order – would greatly improve the accuracy of the input to the supplier's MPC system. The MPS would start with order information that was much firmer than forecasts, although still susceptible to planning changes. However, experience with the stability of the customer's system and continuous updates would help peg the degree of certainty to the system.

Another useful information exchange would be for the supplier to share inventory information with the customer. Suppose customer ABC is preparing to place an order for a specialized product from supplier XYZ. The configuration of the order must be set before the order can be placed. The components for desired configuration must be available at the time the order is processed if the order is to be acknowledged, built and shipped on time. An alternative configuration, using available materials, might be agreed upon when the customer is notified about the delay created by material unavailability. However, this communication between marketing, engineering and materials with the customer may take a long time. A possible solution would be to create an online file, accessible to the customer, that gives the available-to-promise quantities of key components common to most configurations. The customer could then determine in advance whether he wished to submit an order for an alternative configuration or wait for the missing materials to become available.

A third information exchange would be for the customer to share inventory information with the supplier. Order placement for stock replenishment could become the responsibility of the supplier. By monitoring the customer's on-hand balance and considering historical use, logistical data and other inventory data, the supplier could trigger orders and send them to the customer. This could eliminate the customer's need to place purchase orders and minimize demand management activities such as forecasting by passing these responsibilities on to the supplier. This process is usually referred to as vendor- or supplier-managed inventory (VMI or SMI).

Most of these exchanges can be effected by using electronic data interchange (EDI). The best option would be to establish data linkages through a common system, such as the Internet. In some cases, the host organization might break down its firewall and share its internal system. Additional training might be necessary for organizations using the host's system(s). Benefits of information-sharing would be gained through reduction in the uncertainty that exists in system inputs, such as using knowledge of probable orders rather than forecasting. An additional benefit would be cost savings from automating purchasing and related transactions through the system interfaces, such as a reduction in the personnel needed to prepare and monitor purchase orders. The improved flow of information should also result in better customer service based on measures such as on-time delivery (see Figure 10.1).

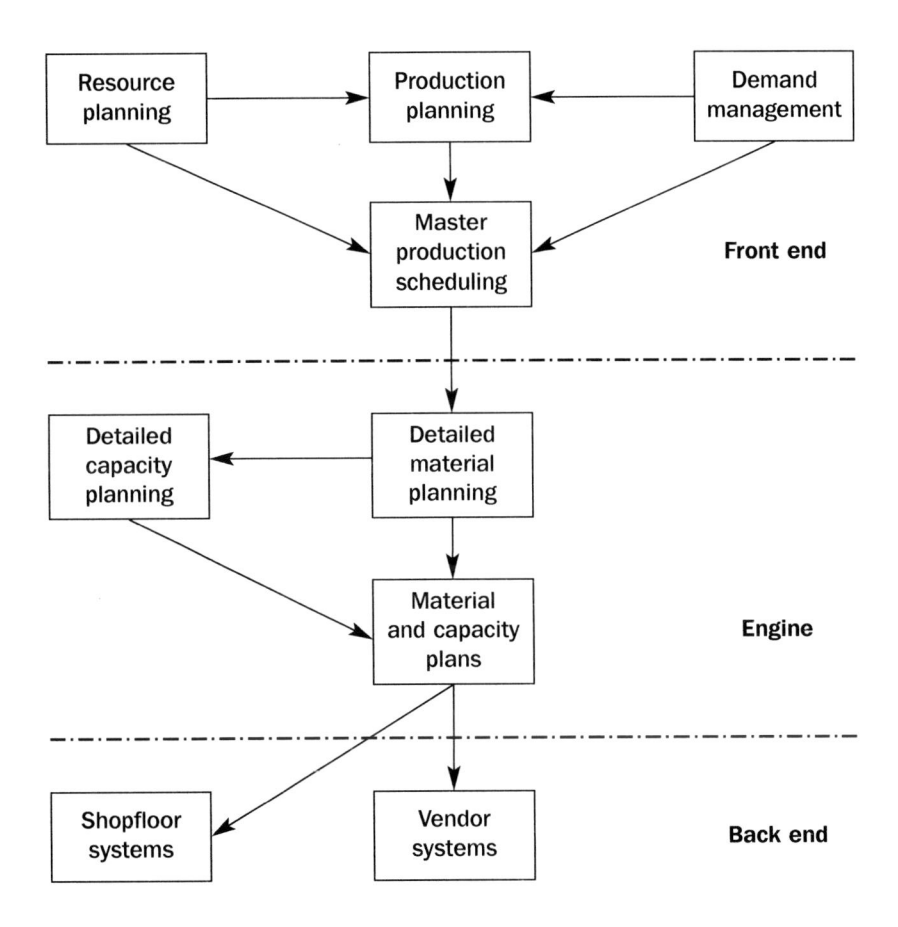

Figure 10.1 Improved flow of information.

CHAPTER 11

Profitability analysis

Why prepare a profitability improvement plan?

Why should your business have a profitability improvement plan? A profitability improvement plan is like a map. There are several ways to get from A to B. The question is, which way is the best? Which is the most efficient? Which is the safest? Your profitability improvement plan provides you with a map to take your business from A to B. Like a map, your profitability improvement plan becomes an ongoing working document. It will need updating from time to time, but will be a great help in addressing the weaknesses and capitalizing on the strengths of your business.

The process of creating a profitability improvement plan forces you to take a realistic, detached look at your whole business. Why is it so important to see your venture as a whole? Most people who have business ideas deal with them in an disorganized manner.

Putting together a profitability improvement plan and writing down specifics provides you with the opportunity to evaluate your business as a whole so that you can then proceed to implement it.

A finished profitability improvement plan becomes an operating tool that will help you manage your business and work toward its success. The final, completed plan is the chief instrument for communicating your ideas to others – business people, bankers, partners, etc. If you seek financing for your business, the plan will become the basis for your loan proposal. The plan allows you to take nebulous thoughts and put them in concrete form.

The importance of planning cannot be overemphasized. It is the key to unlocking the door to success. A profitability improvement plan will give you enough information to help you spot problems before they arise. Planning will help you determine how you can best achieve your business goals.

How your profitability plan can help you

It will:

- help you identify your objectives;

- help you develop strategies to meet those objectives;

- help you earmark problems and suggest ways to solve them;

- help you avoid problems altogether;

- help you obtain the necessary financing for your business.

For a plan to be effective, it is imperative that you do as much of the work, research and investigation of your business as possible. In short, you must do the planning and by devoting the time to organize and write your plan, it will help you to understand better just what your business is capable of doing and will make you a better manager.

When you thoroughly research and pull together your profitability improvement plan, you get an enormous amount of financial and operational information about your business. Information promotes business knowledge and confidence. Confidence, in turn, promotes enthusiasm and makes you the best salesperson for your business. If you are going to use your profitability improvement plan for the purpose of raising money for your business, you will have to be able to sell your idea, your plan and your business. You must take plenty of time to put your plan together correctly. The complexity and size of your profitability improvement plan will reflect the nature and size of your business. If your business is relatively small then the profitability improvement plan will be straightforward but still comprehensive and informative. If your business is large, then your profitability improvement plan will have to be more elaborate and detailed. One thing to remember, however, is that regardless of the size or type of business you have or propose to have, the profitability improvement plan will be written in such a way that an uninformed reader will be able to understand your business and what you are proposing to accomplish.

A good profitability improvement plan will give you important information. A well-organized plan will tell you if your idea makes sense. It can tell the entrepreneur whether there is enough net profit in a business to make it an enterprise worth his time or investment or both. A profitability improvement plan forces you to analyse your market both from your point of view as a business operator and from your potential customer's point of view. You must determine the potential demand for the product or service you plan to offer and, therefore, the plan will tell you whether your idea has a chance in the marketplace.

Who uses profitability improvement plans?

Profitability improvement plans can be used by three groups: you (the applicant), lending institutions and investors (or partners). Each group will look at the profitability improvement plan from a different viewpoint and for different reasons. Each wants to know what is going to be done, when it is going to be done, how it is going to be done and what the final outcome will be.

The owner should be the prime user of the profitability improvement plan. While you may have strong marketing or production skills, how good are you in other areas such as finance, personnel or inventory control? In the preparation of a comprehensive profitability improvement plan you must deal with every aspect affecting your business. As time goes on, the profitability improvement plan should be constantly reviewed and updated to reflect ongoing changes and needs of the operation.

Lending institutions will be interested in how you can repay your loan and provide adequate security. These areas should be carefully explained to answer potential questions. If the profitability improvement plan will be submitted to investors or partners, they will generally want high earnings and a good return for their investment, and will also want to know how and when they will get their money back from the business. Address all these issues very clearly.

Components of the profitability improvement plan

Business development assessment questionnaire

The following questionnaire is designed to identify the potential for profit improvement in your business. It will also give an indication of how to assess your profit improvement potential.

Industry trends

What are the annual sales, in dollars, of your industry or field?
_____

How large will it be in five years? _____

Is this industry growing, stable or declining? _____

Is your industry dominated by a few large companies or many small ones? _____

How likely is it that new companies will enter the industry?
_____

What effect are regulatory or legal issues likely to have on this industry? _____

What important economic events could affect this industry?
_____

What effect are cultural trends (lifestyles, demographics) likely to have on this industry? _____

What technological changes could affect this industry?
_____

Are other products, services or substitutes like yours already offered in this industry? _____

How does your business fit into the industry? _____

What are the average sales and profits for your type of business?

_____

What is the gross margin (sales minus cost of items sold) as a percentage of sales? _____

What are the average expenses as a percentage of sales?

_____

What is the average net profit (sales minus all expenses) as a percentage of sales? _____

What is the normal mark-up (currency mark-up divided by cost of merchandise) as a percentage? _____

What is the annual inventory turnover rate (total sales divided by average inventory value)? _____

For the following questions, circle the correct answer, or the answer that is closest to being correct for you.

Number of competitors in your industry:	Many	Some	Few
Is your industry dominated by a few large firms?		Yes	No
The combined market share of the three largest firms in your industry is:	<40%	40–80%	>80%

New technologies change the way business is done in your industry every:	1 year	5 years	10 years
Barriers that stop new competitors from entering your industry are:	High	Medium	Low
Barriers that prevent exit are:	High	Medium	Low
Overall market demand for your industry is:	Growing	Stable	Declining
Is there a large, untapped market that your industry can take advantage of?		Yes	No
What kind of selection of product lines does your industry offer?	Extensive	Average	Limited
Do customers buy products in your industry based almost entirely on price?		Yes	No
Do customers find substitutes for your industry's products:	Easily	With difficulty	Not at all
Do suppliers to your industry have a lot of power when it comes to setting terms?		Yes	No

Do customers have a lot of bargaining power when buying your industry's products?	Yes	No	
Do distributors have a lot of power in your industry?	Yes	No	
Overall costs in your industry have been:	Declining	Stable	Rising
Profit margins in your industry are:	Strong	Average	Weak

Your business

How many years have you been running this business? _____

How many years have you been involved in owning or managing any business? _____

Did you start this business or did you acquire it?	Started	Acquired
Are you happy with the financial return you're getting from the business?	Yes	No

If you answered 'no', what return would you like to be getting?
_____

On average, how many hours in a typical week do you spend working in your business? _____

How many hours would you like to spend working in your business? _____

What do you consider to be the biggest problems in your business? (Rank the items in the table below in order of their importance from 1 to 16, where 1 = most critical problem and 16 = least critical problem.) Ignore items if they are not applicable.

Lack of capital for expansion		Price competition	
Lack of sales		Lack of time to do what needs to be done	
Cash flow		Not enough customers	
Slow-paying customers		Supplier problems	
Lack of skilled people		Production problems	
Difficulty getting employees focused		Government regulations	
Difficulty hiring suitable managers		State of the economy	
Taxation		Other (specify)	

If you had access to unlimited finance, what would you do to improve the business?

_____

_____

What key performance indicators do you use to monitor the progress of your business?

_____

_____

Do you set targets as a reference point
for managing your business?   Yes   No

Do you have a business action plan that sets out precisely what you need to do to achieve your profit target?　　　　Yes　　　No

In the list below, tick all those you involve in critical decision making in your business.

Board of directors		External businesses	
Employed managers		Your spouse	
Other employees		Friends	
Your accountant		Other (specify)	
Your lawyer			

What was the main reason you went into business for yourself?

_____

_____

Do you feel you are achieving the above reason? If 'no', please explain why.

_____

_____

In five years, what is your target for (please complete table below):

	Target	Don't know
Revenue		
Net profit		
Number of employees		
Number of employees now		

What is the value of your business now? _____ Don't know

What would you like your business to be worth in five years? _____ Don't know

Do you have a strategic plan to help you achieve that goal?   Yes   No

How much money have you invested in your business?

	Amount
Equity capital	
Loans to the business	
Value of personal property mortgaged to secure business loans	
Total exposure	

To assess your profit improvement potential, please provide the following information. (*Note:* If you do not know your exact average transaction value, an estimate is fine at this stage. Give a reasonable estimate by picking 20 sales invoices at random and calculating the average. If you feel comfortable that the result is about right, enter the value in the space provided below. If you're still unsure, select more invoices until you're confident that your estimate gives a fair indication of the true average.)

What is your average transaction value? _____

Do you have a system to measure this, or is it estimated?

_____

How many times a year do your average customers buy from you (tick the correct answer from the list below)?

PROFITABILITY ANALYSIS

Once a year		Once a week	
Once a quarter		Once a day	
Once a month		Other (specify)	

How many active customers do you have? _____ Don't know

Do you have a system to measure this, or is it estimated?

_____

Product line analysis

Perform a product line analysis by picking the top 20 and mid 20 sales invoices and calculating the margins of each. If you feel comfortable that the profit margins are about right, enter the value in the spaces in the table below.

	Top 20	*Mid 20*
Total revenue		
Gross profit		
Total expenses		
Other income (expense)		
Net profit before tax		
Other information:		
Number of employees		
Total salaries and wages		
Total interest charges		
Total depreciation		

Business process analysis

Perform an analysis of each business process listed below to see whether you've covered each area adequately.

General operations
1. Establish primary goals of the company – maintenance of status quo, evaluation and recommendations or take charge through implementation of new game plan.
2. Meet all managers, introduce game plan and initiate implementation of action items on this list.
3. Have all managers complete the agenda for the future.
4. Discuss the dozen biggest problems and opportunities from the perspective of all first-reports.
5. If survival mode is required, cut costs immediately where necessary and prudent and in accordance with the company's short- and medium-term goals.
6. Identify and implement top six action items that could measurably increase short-term revenues.
7. In addition to this action list, formulate a short-term game plan for the company, get company approval and communicate plan to key personnel, suppliers, lenders, etc.
8. Prioritize top ten action items for the whole company and begin implementation.
9. Identify top goals for the company for the current month, quarter and year.
10. Set up forecasts so that they provide early warning of potential risks/opportunities vs. reports against budgeted targets – revise forecasts on an exception base only and through a single common tool.

11. Focus forecast analysis and reporting on tactical plan adjustments to meet budget.

Financial issues
1. Within the first week, get current detailed financial statements, itemized payroll, payables and receivables list.
2. Review budgets of all departments or divisions for reasonableness of assumptions, quality of projections and relevancy in light of recent corporate changes and goals.
3. Evaluate obvious, and not so obvious, problems and strengths revealed by the financial statements.
4. Do realistic cash forecast for the next 90- and 180-day periods.
5. Evaluate asset utilization and redeploy if appropriate and prudent in the short term.
6. Review banking and debt obligations for next 90-, 180- and 365-day periods and ensure no technical or major defaults, if possible. If in default, develop game plan and/or negotiate workout.
7. Determine which critical suppliers have suspended support due to lack of payment or other problems.
8. Identify and take steps to immediately defuse all 'time bombs'.
9. Know margins by customer and product.
10. Understand your process costs and cost drivers.
11. Develop customer P&Ls.
12. Prioritize opportunities – develop a customer profit plan.

Supply chain management
1. Manage areas such as accounts receivable, accounts payable, inventory turns and cash to cash cycle time to improve working capital efficiency.

2. Manage return on assets, capacity and throughput, and network optimization and outsourcing to improve fixed capital efficiency.
3. Keep supply chain costs low through process cost reductions, shared services and outsourcing without jeopardizing customer satisfaction.
4. Minimize the company's tax rates by managing asset location, sales locations, transfer prices and customs duties.
5. Ensure profitability through new product development, maintaining a global presence, good after-sales service and perfect order fulfilment.

Regulatory/legal/litigation
1. Ensure all payroll taxes are paid and properly reported.
2. Determine what, if any, problems exist with your country's tax collection service.
3. Ensure the company is in compliance with all required regulatory and licensing agencies, etc. and if not, take action to resolve these issues.
4. Identify all outstanding legal issues and litigation risks along with probable, and possible, associated costs.
5. Ensure no securities law violations have occurred. If they have, take immediate steps to remedy them or mitigate their impact.
6. Ensure any patents, trade secrets, trademarks and copyrights are properly filed and that appropriate protections are in place.

Product lines/marketing/sales/distribution: know your customers' needs
1. Analyse product delivery schedules and takes steps to improve meeting commitment dates.

2. Evaluate product development timetables, budget forecasts and quality of project management systems, procedures and controls.
3. Evaluate sales, marketing, distribution, forecasts and trend lines for improvement opportunities in all areas so as to generate more cash in the short term.
4. Identify both the best customers and the most unhappy customers, as well as the company's image in the marketplace.
5. Complete competitive analyses for each product line.
6. Evaluate pricing models for each product line and adjust accordingly.
7. Identify product line strengths and weaknesses and develop short-term action plans to solve the worst problems.
8. Identify potential products – 6, 12 and 24 months into the future – and their possible impact on revenue and expenses.
9. Establish/update/expand web presence.
10. Evaluate expenditures and effectiveness of marketing and advertising for media, trade shows, market research, focus groups and public relations, and adjust accordingly.
11. Evaluate sales force, sales-related incentives, sales targets, sales personnel training, special offers, dealerships, telemarketing and sales support.
12. Evaluate and optimize short-term inventory.
13. Evaluate customer/technical support, warranties, guarantees and after-sales service.

Personnel issues

1. Upon arrival, communicate with all company personnel for introduction and conveyance of immediate game plan.

2. Set up suggestion boxes, and invite anonymous e-mail, to gain insight into less obvious underlying problems.
3. Review major human resource department aspects of company for legal compliance, competitiveness of benefits package, diversity, clarity of policies and potential cost savings.
4. Evaluate strengths and weaknesses of all first reports.
5. Develop 30-/60-/90-day performance plans for all managers.
6. Evaluate organizational structure and effectiveness – and reorganize if appropriate, adjusting total payroll if necessary.
7. Identify best and worst five per cent of employees in the company, replacing worst five per cent and ensuring the best five per cent are motivated enough to stay.
8. Analyse employee turnover rates to identify main problem areas.
9. Identify key personnel and unfilled job functions, define criteria and initiate search, within budget constraints.
10. Identify personality issues/company policies that may be creating a negative impact on company morale and productivity.
11. Review/modify written delegation of authority for all managers.
12. Review all employment contracts or agreements, both oral and written, including any severance or termination compensation agreements with salaried, hourly or collectively bargaining employees.
13. Review all bonus, deferred compensation, stock option, profit sharing, retirement programmes or plans covering salaried, hourly or collectively bargaining employees.

IPO/merger/acquisition/disposition/dissolution
1. Identify which mergers, acquisitions, dispositions and investments make the most sense for the company.
2. Identify the growth issues regarding acquisitions, spin-offs, expansion and downsizing, as well as closing existing branches and plant.
3. If decision is to sell the company, establish price and terms, subject to company approval, prepare sales summary and develop game plan and methodology for sale.
4. Complete three-year pro forma, based on realistic assumptions, to determine future valuation potential of company and likelihood of IPO or merger/acquisition potential.
5. If company decision is to dissolve company, develop game plan for liquidation of assets and/or follow up on bankruptcy filing.

General/administrative
1. Evaluate and control travel, entertainment and all discretionary expenditures and implement new written policies for these issues.
2. Review facilities and real estate issues, including a review of current lease requirements.
3. Review all equipment leases for cost-cutting/improved technology opportunities.
4. Create/update business plan for current internal clarity and banking or capital formation needs.
5. 'Manage by roaming around', gaining insights into attitudes and problem areas in all levels of the organization.
6. Evaluate in-place systems and procedures and streamline where appropriate.

7. Evaluate technology implementation and optimize within budget constraints.
8. Visit all branch offices and evaluate their needs, performance, personnel and cost-effectiveness.

Stockholder status/investor relations
1. Evaluate investor and stockholder relations and communication status, and initiate appropriate action.
2. Generate updated lists of all current shareholders and percentage ownership of each.
3. Review stock options or purchase plans and agreements, as well as lists of outstanding warrants and options, including date of grant, exercise price, number of shares subject to option and date of exercise.

Environmental, safety and risk management
1. Establish an approved and documented environmental policy for your company.
2. Ensure that all relevant environmental legislation is complied with.
3. Identify, monitor and manage all environmental measures on an ongoing basis.
4. Ensure that all risks are identified, assessed and covered.
5. Ensure that insurance costs are competitive and represent good value for money.
6. Ensure that all insurance claims are accurately assessed, costed and settled.
7. Ensure that measures are in place to prevent the following: unauthorized access to company premises; theft of company

property; damage or disruption caused by vandalism, burglary and other security threats.
8. Define and assess potential risks and security threats.
9. Establish documented procedures for emergency drills, building evacuations and contingency arrangements. Assess their effectiveness.
10. Identify and address all health and safety risks in the organization.
11. Ensure that staff are fully aware of workplace risks and can use safety equipment correctly.
12. Update safety equipment on a regular basis, ensure that it is regularly maintained, and ensure that staff are capable of using it correctly.
13. Put in place adequate fire prevention systems and test them regularly.
14. Provide adequate first aid, medical, hygiene and cleanliness facilities.
15. Ensure that all incidents and accidents are reported in a timely fashion and are appropriately dealt with.
16. Ensure that all hazardous materials are safely, correctly and securely stored.

Follow-up

Report to the company the status of the company, your evaluation, recommended modifications to the short-term game plan, and any cash needs.

CHAPTER 12

Conclusion

All good business owners and managers know they should have a solid, working business plan in place. However, for the business operator, taking the time to write a profitability business plan is easier said than done. It seems there are always more pressing problems to tackle.

But the truth is that a business owner or manager will never reach total success unless she draws a map of how she plans to get there. That map or business plan will provide direction on how to move toward attaining business goals and, ultimately, success. A well-developed plan also helps when a business encounters sharp curves in the road, a bumpy stretch of highway or even a pothole that temporarily derails its progress. While these road conditions may impede success, they need not be devastating. By thinking about profitability plans while preparing a profitability business plan, a business owner or manager can be prepared to handle the ups and downs of the business world.

Generally, most businesses do their profitability planning on a yearly basis. Once a plan has been developed, it can be reviewed, revised and refocused annually as needed. It's important for the plan to include a business's long-term goals and projections. For a start-up business, a long-term plan may only cover the next six months, while that of a large corporation may span the next five or even ten years. A three- to five-year profitability plan is standard for most established businesses.

The first step in any profitability business plan is writing a mission statement, a responsibility usually reserved for the owner or manager of a business. The goal is to keep the statement as short as possible so that employees understand and remember it. The statement can be as simple as, 'Our mission is to make money'. In fact, businesses always should include some reference to profitability in their mission statements. Step 2 of the profitability business plan includes both internal and external assessments. In the internal assessment, a business owner or manager should examine the history of the business and where the business has come from. Some of the internal factors to gauge are financial information, operational information, business facilities, products and services, market share, customer profiles, marketing efforts and human resources issues. In the external assessment, a business owner or manager should consider how external factors have affected his business in the past and also how they may affect business in the future. This is when profitability plans first enter the profitability planning picture. At this point, a business operator should think about how the business can weather or even benefit from changing external factors, those beyond his control.

Probably the most important external factor that impacts any business is competition. It is critical for a business owner or manager to thoroughly assess its competitors in terms of who they are, what products and services they offer, where their customer base is and how well they're doing. A good rule to follow is: know a competitor's business at least as well as your own.

Once the business analysis has been done, it's time to identify your business's strengths, weaknesses, opportunities and threats in a SWOT analysis. To complete this part of the profitability plan, a business owner or manager may want to ask other key employees to take part in a brainstorming session where lists are made. Profitability planning falls under the Threats category. Begin by thinking about events or situations that could come out of the blue and adversely affect your business. A business owner or manager who fails to do this can also fail to react to sudden changes in the business environment because of the economy, the competition or other factors. For example, today's low interest rates are extremely advantageous to businesses that need to borrow money for expansion. How will a business survive if interest rates suddenly double? The first step is to address this potential threat and create a profitability plan to deal with it. In this example, the profitability plan may include locking into a long-term, fixed interest rate.

The fourth step in the profitability planning process is identifying four or five critical issues that may impact business. These are usually one- or two-word issues, such as profitability, product or service quality, business development, training or employee relations. While a business owner or manager could probably name many more, it's better to focus on a few issues that can be targeted for improvement during the plan year.

Step 5 is stating the desired position of the business in a given time frame. In this portion of the profitability plan, a business owner or manager should refer back to each of the critical issues identified and ask, 'Where do I want my business to be in terms of profitability in three years?' By answering that question, she sets goals. Perhaps she wants to increase profitability by 50 per cent during the next three years. Now the business has a specific goal to strive for and, more importantly, a way to measure its success. Keep this advice in mind: if a goal isn't measured, it probably won't be accomplished.

Devising strategies is the final phase of the business plan. A business owner or manager should refer again to each of the critical issues and the goals set for them in Step 5. This time the question is, 'What can we do to ensure that our goals are met?' Using the profitability example, possible answers may be cutting costs and increasing sales. Then go one step further by asking another question: 'How are we going to achieve our goals?' The answers to this question become the basis for the business operational plan. For example, to achieve profitability, a business owner or manager may decide to find alternative suppliers in order to cut costs, and identify potential new customers in order to increase sales. At this point, it's important for a business owner or manager to involve all employees in the profitability plan by assigning them certain responsibilities for attaining business goals and by making sure they understand where the business is headed. This empowers employees to do their best work and ultimately makes the business more successful.

While profitability plans are an important element of the profitability planning process, it may be best to include them in a separate, but adjoining, document. Business owners and managers who focus too much on business problems or failures in their plans may never do what is really needed to achieve success. On the other hand, business owners and managers who ignore profitability planning have their heads in the sand. They aren't facing up to the ever-changing and challenging reality of the business world.

This book considered how we analyse global/financial/operational information to help understand a company's competitive strategy. In addition, we learned how to determine whether the chosen strategy has been successfully implemented to create value for owners. We also considered the relationship between cost behaviour and profitability. Gaining an understanding of how costs and revenues respond to changes in activity helps managers to make better operating and investing decisions. There are no standard approaches or solutions to working in zones of conflict. None of the solutions is especially complicated, nor are they costly or based on specialized expertise. What they do require is that corporate and local plant managers recognize the ways in which their decisions can reduce or worsen conflict. This kind of examination and understanding can create stronger overall business stability.

Companies that are experiencing high growth, competition, lack of skilled resources and significant changes in organization, process and technology are under pressure. A business profitability programme should facilitate success in these areas. A commitment to an ongoing profitability programme will yield consistent results in the long term. These results include improved revenues, market share and profits. However, these results may take years to surface and the reason for the improvement could be inhibited by other influences. Other more immediate, although less tangible, benefits not only address these issues but may be used as an early warning measure of what the bottom-line benefits will be. To ensure that these benefits are realized, the management team must support an ongoing programme of business profitability and see to it that the necessary enablers are in place.

APPENDIX A

Product realization checklist

1. Is the project well aligned with the business plans and the management plans?
2. Has an adequate business case analysis been performed and are the results well documented and available?
3. Is the business case based on the full cost of the system from initiation through to implementation and estimated annual cost of operation?
4. Has the project sponsor, representing the users, taken accountability and responsibility for project scope and definition?
5. Have the requirements been reviewed and approved by the project sponsor?
6. Are there formal, documented plans in place to involve appropriate levels of users throughout the project (from requirements definition through evaluation and acceptance of deliverables, product and integration testing to final acceptance and sign-off)?

7. Has the project sponsor ensured user commitment and support?
8. Is the project justification based on an ROI with a good projected return?
9. Are the project specifications defined?
10. Is there agreement from all executives that the project is essential (either to support something else you are doing or for future positioning)?

Accountability
1. Are the positions of project sponsor, project leader and project manager filled?
2. Are there clearly defined, documented and understood responsibilities, accountabilities and authorities for each of these positions?
3. Is the matrix defining the accountabilities, responsibilities and authorities appropriate for this project?
4. If there is a need for a project manager representing a contractor, are there clearly defined, documented (beyond the contract) and understood responsibilities, accountabilities and authorities for this position?
5. Has the project manager identified adequate resources to allocate to the scheduled tasks at the scheduled time?
6. Does the staff have sufficient expertise in the project domain?
7. Is the project sponsor at the correct level in the organization? Will this executive be held accountable for delivering the benefits outlined in the proposal?
8. Have the project team and the organization successfully implemented a project of similar size, scope, cost or duration?

9. Is the project within the demonstrated capability of the department and contractors?
10. Do status/progress meetings occur regularly?
11. Are issues raised and dealt with?
12. Is this project on time and on budget?
13. Are changes in scope being managed?
14. Are adequate staff allocated to the scheduled tasks at the scheduled times?
15. Have all key players lived up to their accountabilities and responsibilities? If not, has this been addressed?
16. Are the contractor's project management activities periodically reviewed by the project manager?
17. Have the project manager and project sponsor previously managed a project of this size, scope and complexity?
18. Does the project manager have sufficient control over appropriate project resources?
19. Does the project manager have the freedom and ability to act when warranted?
20. Is the project manager prepared to escalate issues when warranted, based on predetermined criteria?
21. Is the escalation path clear and documented?
22. Is the necessary information available to support decisive action?
23. Is the project independent of other projects which are presently underway (i.e. not relying on the successful completion of other projects)?

Risk management
1. Was a formal process used to break down the work and estimate task duration?

2. Are formal mechanisms or tools in place to monitor the project schedule?
3. Are costs allocated in accordance with work breakdown structures?
4. Do team leaders sign-off on cost and schedule estimates, and are they held to budgetary constraints?
5. Have all known management and technical risks been assessed, and are mitigation strategies in place for all identified risks?
6. Does the project approach pass reasonable checks for what is to be accomplished?
7. Can the project manager and sponsor list the current top ten project risks?
8. Is the technology being used well tested and have project staff got sufficient experience in using it?
9. Is it reasonable to expect financial stability for the duration of the project?
10. Were all risks identified and managed properly?
11. Were the mechanisms and tools used to monitor the project schedule adequate?
12. Were team leaders held to budgetary constraints?
13. Was there adequate communication with all involved personnel throughout the project?
14. Did the contractor provide necessary information on project performance and progress?
15. Did the project reviews (including internal/external peer reviews) occur as scheduled?
16. Was there enough time, money and resources to get the job done right?

17. Were there adequate contingency plans for potential problems (i.e. no problems arose for which there were no contingency plans)?
18. Had the project complexity been accurately determined before start-up?
19. Were all changes analysed quickly and brought to management's attention in a timely fashion?

Support for the business
1. Has the project sponsor, representing the users, taken responsibility for keeping the project within scope?
2. Has the project sponsor ensured user commitment throughout the project (from evaluation and acceptance of deliverables, product and integration testing to final acceptance and sign-off)?
3. Have the business goals for the organization changed and, if so, is the new system still aligned with the goals of the organization?
4. Has the business case been reviewed and revalidated at each scheduled gate?
5. Has the business case been reviewed and revalidated whenever there was significant change to the project or business function?
6. If the business case has changed, has project re-approval been sought by the department?
7. If project specifications have changed significantly, have these changes been well documented and approved by the appropriate stakeholders?
8. Were all issues resolved in a timely fashion and to everyone's satisfaction?

9. Did the project finish on time and within budget?
10. Was the project adequately staffed during all phases?
11. Were issues with respect to weak or poorly performing personnel quickly and adequately addressed?
12. Was a project wrap-up session held to document 'lessons learned'?
13. Did the project sponsor assume responsibility for realizing the benefits predicted for the project?
14. Did the project leader assume responsibility and accountability for all aspects of the project (internal and external)?
15. Did the project achieve all its defined objectives?

Corporate project manager discipline
1. In the event of serious problems, has the necessary information been available to support decisive action?
2. In the event of serious problems, have the necessary decisions been taken promptly?
3. Are the procurement, contracting and security issues being dealt with?
4. Is the project maintaining a positive image (i.e. there are no rumours that the project is in trouble)?
5. Is the project manager avoiding premature and inappropriate use of contingency funding?
6. Is the project manager maintaining sufficient control over appropriate project resources?
7. Is the contractor providing complete information on project performance and progress?
8. Are project managers going to others in the organization for advice and support?

9. Have any new risks surfaced, and are they being properly addressed?
10. Is it still reasonable to expect financial stability for the remainder of the project?
11. Have there been minimal changes to the organization or the business since project initiation?
12. Are the formal mechanisms and tools used to monitor the project schedule adequate?
13. Are the team leaders being held to budgetary constraints?
14. Does the management approach continue to ensure coordination of all sub-projects, ensure communication among different sub-project teams, and address shared horizontal issues?
15. Are internal/external peer reviews being held as scheduled?
16. Are oversight reviews by a senior steering committee being carried out at each gate?
17. Are regular sessions held to review the continued relevance of the project and project performance, and to raise concerns about actual/potential problems?

Client support
1. Were the clients involved throughout the project from evaluation and acceptance of deliverables, product and integration testing to final acceptance and sign-off?
2. Were all types of clients represented in the project?
3. Did the clients carry through on their commitment to the level of effort required of them?
4. Were clients satisfied with the final deliverable?
5. Was the final product aligned with the goals of the organization?

6. Did the project remain within the predefined scope?
7. Were any changes to project specifications documented and approved by stakeholders?
8. Was the project consistent and compatible with the department's information technology direction, strategies, architectures and infrastructures?

APPENDIX B

Cost savings analysis

Take the time to assess your company using the following analysis, which is designed to identify the potential for profit improvement in your business.

Business efficiency methods

Planning

- Review operating statements and identify areas that offer best cost reduction potential
- Flow chart all major areas
- Group related functions under the same supervision
- Shorten the chain of command
- Define responsibilities and authority; eliminate overlaps
- Decentralize and/or centralize operations as appropriate

- Develop a profit planning programme for employees
- Measure benefits before spending
- Make employees plan major jobs in advance of implementation
- Defer all new actions until true needs are determined
- Reduce all committees and the length of each meeting
- Have an annual cost reduction suggestion programme

Analyses of departments and activities

- Are all departments necessary? Should any be added?
- Are all jobs necessary?
- Are company-sponsored organizations necessary?
- Establish a word-processing centre
- Reduce central filing
- Centralize office services
- Evaluate all major cost programmes

Personnel

- Set a good example for your staff
- Promote from within to improve morale
- Institute a hiring freeze for short periods
- Review manpower requirements periodically
- Review all education and training programmes
- Have periodic performance reviews
- Request periodic time distribution reports from employees

Efficiency

- Start and leave work on time
- Utilize people to full capacity and qualifications
- Permit carryover of work load and level out peaks
- Reduce overtime by better scheduling and prioritizing work
- Review all form designs for efficiency
- Review quality of office equipment
- Standardize equipment
- Use more estimates in accounting
- Eliminate business and trade reports when not necessary
- Establish convenient libraries for manuals
- Use combination requisition, purchase order and receiving reports
- Route reports rather than prepare multiple report copies
- Use microfilm files to save space
- Use computer to assist auditors
- Use cheaper paper in photocopiers
- Cut down on waste
- Reduce duplicating by use of shared computer files
- Utilize photocopiers at strategic locations
- Establish a form control manual; control quantities of forms
- Review all forms for necessity and simplicity
- Review all stationery costs
- Reduce the size of annual reports and the number of colours used
- Purchase and issue office supplies in economical quantities
- Reduce the kinds of accounting paper carried in inventory
- Control supplies and sundries

Office facilities

- Have more modest offices
- Eliminate offices for lower supervisory personnel
- Use proper wattage and voltage of lighting
- Turn out lights when not in use
- Establish janitorial procedures that cycle the work load
- Remove materials from desk nightly to reduce cleaners' work
- Set standards for floor space allowances by classification of office employees

Outside services

- Hire temporary staff for emergencies; no overtime
- Utilize an auditor's free technical service
- Cut out professional services where possible
- Do your own building maintenance
- Use bank facilities to mechanically reconcile bank accounts

Communications

- Review all communications and facilities
- Start a telephone expense reduction campaign
- Reduce switchboard hours
- Use one central mailroom only
- Install inter-office mail and messenger service
- Mechanize mail processing
- Use lowest class mail rate when feasible
- Use lighter paper and envelopes

- Reuse envelopes for internal mail
- Reduce size of mailing lists
- Don't use express mail unless really necessary

Meetings and travel

- Strictly regulate all travel
- Cut out executive cars
- Cut out company planes
- Use economy instead of first-class air travel
- Use the airport bus instead of taxis
- Stagger company hours to relieve congestion problems
- Lease company cars instead of purchasing
- Set up your own transportation fleet
- Reduce meeting and travel expense by a set percentage
- Eliminate or reduce convention attendance
- Use cheaper hotels
- Make contact travel arrangements with hotels in cities that are frequently visited by company employees
- Control moving expenses of people transferred
- Eliminate expensive stockholder meetings
- Eliminate special stockholder meetings by better planning
- Cut down on lunch meetings
- Have management meetings at corporate offices

Payroll and fringe benefits

- Schedule overtime by priority
- Dock employees for being late

- Have shorter lunch breaks
- Have pay deposited into employees' bank accounts
- Schedule varying pay rates to level load in the payroll department and reduce staff
- Eliminate fringe benefits – picnics, golf outings, etc.
- Review employee stock option plans
- Eliminate Christmas gifts to employees
- Eliminate or reduce coffee breaks
- Have suggestion awards programmes

Funds

- Raise capitalization limits
- Keep petty cash funds to a minimum
- Minimize the number of bank accounts
- Review discount procedures
- Hold payables for maximum but pay for discount
- Have salesmen and drivers deposit collections directly into banks

Taxes and insurance

- Move to lower tax areas
- Control inventories to reduce property taxes
- Don't pay tax until it's due
- Establish subsidiary corporations for branches in areas that tax on the total company business
- Review insurance costs
- Negotiate insurance rates on a package basis

Subscriptions and dues

- Reduce memberships of outside societies, clubs and associations
- Eliminate duplicate memberships in organizations
- Buy industrial or trade magazines at wholesale prices
- Centralize magazine services
- Reduce the number of magazine and newspaper subscriptions
- Develop bibliography of current periodicals to ensure review of latest ideas

Miscellaneous

- Assemble all reports into a single manual
- Establish greater security to avoid inventory thefts
- Obtain competitive bids for purchases of materials and supplies
- Review technical magazines systematically for cost-saving ideas
- Develop checklist of cost-saving and profit-producing approaches with key staff members

Product engineering

- Eliminate need for a specific part
- Substitute a cheaper material
- Reduce the number of parts needed
- Combine part functions
- Design for low-cost tooling
- Design for high-speed production
- Increase feeds and speeds
- Reduce the number of design changes

- Design to reduce scrap
- Design to standardize production processes
- Use standard hardware in place of custom hardware
- Design to reduce manual production operations
- Design to reduce material content
- Design to reduce the number of fasteners required
- Use specific alloys to enable faster machining
- Use specific alloys to cut tool wear
- Design the cheapest finish feasible

Shipping, receiving and warehousing

- Use conveyors for moving operations
- Use reusable pallets and storage boxes
- Keep warehouse locked
- Minimize travel distances
- Group like parts together in warehouse
- Use hydraulic lifts instead of ladders
- Ship and receive in unit loads
- Protect products from damage and corrosion
- Use maximum height for warehouse storage
- Speed up handling through improved scheduling
- Use proper storage containers
- Prearrange movement of materials
- Replace obsolete equipment
- Combine clerical operations
- Place fastest-moving items near dock
- Mechanize all movement of material

- Keep aisle space down to minimum needs
- Practise first in-first out
- Properly identify all stock
- Check all freight rates/bills
- Use economical small package ship methods
- Unload promptly
- Keep bills of lading legible
- Count number of parts received

Production planning and control

- Reduce the number of product lines
- Reduce the size of purchased lots
- Reduce the size of production lots
- Use better forecasting techniques
- Convert obsolete parts into current production
- Keep inventories organized
- Keep inventory records accurate
- Reduce the number of salaried people needed
- Keep overtime low
- Keep warehouse space filled
- Reduce office space
- Reduce overhead expenses
- Improve package design
- Keep written procedures current
- Keep work standards up to date
- Shrink lead times
- Reduce emergency orders

- Keep production routings up to date
- Provide fast access to stock
- Use effective communications systems
- Minimize material flow
- Maintain forklift trucks in good order
- Improve inspection techniques
- Improve vendor performance
- Guard against incorrect engineering drawings
- Provide for scrap/rework when planning
- Schedule to minimize waiting time
- Renegotiate vendor prices
- Keep production overruns to a minimum
- Recognize production bottlenecks, then minimize them
- Keep accurate records
- Load work centres to minimize set-ups
- Minimize sales changes to the master schedule

Plant and manufacturing engineering

- Correct wrong bills of materials
- Reduce average earnings
- Curtail use of fuel and electricity
- Correct loose work standards
- Keep 90 per cent of all production jobs on standard
- Keep 80 per cent of all indirect labour jobs on standard
- Use allowances in standards sparingly
- Ensure the proper use of feeds and speeds

- Issue frequent labour performance reports
- Combine production operations
- Change standards to reflect improved methods
- Sample production counts for accuracy
- Analyse and reduce machine downtime
- Standardize equipment parts
- Combine or reduce machine set-ups
- Simplify tooling, jigs and fixtures
- Keep accurate and up-to-date equipment records
- Lease rather than buy equipment
- Mechanize manual operations

Quality control

- Reduce scrap levels
- Reduce rework levels
- Reduce warranty
- Improve tool and gauge inspection
- Reduce vendor quality problems
- Calibrate testing equipment
- Prohibit use of marked-up engineering prints
- Scrap all makeshift tooling
- Segregate defective stock
- Modernize inspection equipment
- Review packaging quality
- Investigate sales of plant scrap

Safety

- Establish a plant safety programme
- Get advice on safety issues
- Hire a nurse to screen employees for diseases
- Have workers participate in the safety programme
- Use posters and awards to make employees more safety-conscious
- Get the unions on your side
- Use control reports to monitor progress
- Use accident reports to identify and correct safety problems
- Publish safety rules, and discipline offenders
- Provide safety training for all new employees
- Make safety the responsibility of line managers
- Use self-inspection checklists
- Use an internal expert on safety regulations
- Investigate accident-prone employees
- Provide first aid training for emergencies
- Conduct housekeeping tours to prevent accidents
- Have the plant manager chair the safety committee
- Know how to use fire extinguishers
- Use lead-free paint
- Use safety glasses on every job